There is such a thing as society

Twelve principles of compassionate conservatism

Edited by

Gary Streeter

Published in Great Britain 2002
by Politico's Publishing
8 Artillery Row
Westminster
London
SW1P 1RZ

www.politicos.co.uk/publishing

A catalogue record of this book is available from the British Library.

ISBN 1 84275 054 2

Printed and bound in Great Britain by Creative Print and Design

Contents

v

There is such a thing as society

Part three: Twelve principles of compassionate conservatism

Each principle is introduced by David McLetchie

Contents

Conservatives must change in order to help the vulnerable

Gary Streeter

Gary Streeter is the MP for Devon South West. In his ten years in Parliament he has consistently spoken out on social exclusion and inner city deprivation. He was a minister in John Major's government, Shadow Secretary of State for International Development under William Hague and is currently a Conservative Party vice-chairman with responsibility for the Renewing One Nation team. He is married to Janet and has two children, both at university.

Vulnerable people

A child is born into a dysfunctional home, lacking in stability or encouragement. He attends the local primary school where teachers have become demoralised and anti-social behaviour is rampant. He lacks self-esteem. He may be intelligent but he doesn't sit still long enough for anybody at his failing inner city secondary school to ever find out. As he grows he dabbles in drink and drugs and crime and under-age sex. He gets in a few fights and has an early run-in with the police. He plays truant more often than not, fails his exams at sixteen, cannot wait to leave school, drifts into crime on a more regular basis and fathers a child that he rarely sees.

He is a product of our times. At age five he has already set the pattern for the rest of his life, confirmed and entrenched it by age fifteen. He is an under-achiever. He is on the outside looking in. He will not fulfil his potential.

Who is this child? He is you and I born to a different family. He is you and I born in a different body or a different place. He is you and I having made some bad life choices or fallen in with the wrong crowd. He is destined for a life of frustration and he will cost us all dear in the crime he commits and the welfare his lifestyle consumes. Without real and effective intervention, he is unlikely to break out of the cycles of aspirational poverty that ensnare him. He threatens to bring the whole of our society crashing down on our heads.

This book is about him and our response to him. He is but one example of the countless thousands, maybe millions, of rootless restless young people who fill our towns and cities. It is also about many other people who find themselves excluded from a world that most of us take for granted. It is about the people born with chronic disability. It is about the homeless, the children in care homes, the addicts and the unemployed. It is about the person coasting through life until some unforeseen life shock suddenly places her in need of a helping hand.

We have never had so many laws; never been more materially prosperous; never spent so much money on welfare; never has there been such a vast array of government schemes designed to make life better for the socially excluded. And yet . . . Does any informed commentator genuinely think that after another few more years of this Labour Government and its ever more glitzy centralised initiatives that these deep-seated problems will be significantly ameliorated? I doubt it. But criticising Labour's failure is not enough. How will the Conservative Party help the next generation of vulnerable people? What hope of a better tomorrow will we offer them?

Social breakdown must be the Conservatives' number one priority

The next Conservative Government will face many challenges: our relationship within the European Union; the threat of world terror; the impact of globalisation; the need for reform of the public services. But I suggest that none will be greater than the social challenges of drugs, rising crime, alienation and inter-generational poverty. The child with whom I begin this chapter is not a myth; he is real and one of many.

We must start with a firm determination not to shrink from the challenge. The essays in this book – from the leader of the party and other senior figures – make this very clear. But we must not delude ourselves that this new mission will be easy. The scale of the social challenge is very daunting, similar to the economic battles that faced the incoming Conservative Government of 1979. There will be many who say from behind their secure walls that little can be done; that this is not our battle; or, worse still, we can afford it – let us pay our taxes; employ enough police and social workers to sit on the problem while we get on with the 'real' political issues.

This book is about kicking over the traces; turning things upside down; ripping up the map book of the recent past and turning to another less narrow guide, namely our rich heritage of radical Conservative compassion. The heritage is all there but our telescope is perhaps too short. The problems facing our generation require as radical a reforming social agenda as the diet of effective economic reform served up by the party in the 1980s. Nothing less will do.

The scene is set with two accounts of the true nature of vulnerability in twenty-first-century Britain. We begin in Easterhouse in Glasgow, looking at the entrenched social problems through the eyes of one who has strived to serve the vulnerable for many years. But we go on to demonstrate through a battery of hard-hitting facts that similar problems disfigure all parts of the country. We do not attempt to argue that everyone's life is dogged in this way. Many people are achieving their potential and we celebrate that. There is an obvious temptation for opposition parties to exaggerate defects. For most people life is good: they are doing well at work, enjoy strong relationships, and relaxing leisure time. But the sad reality is that the lives of a vast number of our fellow citizens fall well short of their potential through a complex tangled set of choices and chances. And even many comfortable people are only a few life shocks away from serious challenges. This is as unsustainable as it is unnecessary.

In the twelve essays written by grassroots members of the party, we see many new ideas and different approaches to tackling some of these issues. The titles of the essays outline twelve important principles that can help inform our debate. I do not seek to summarise them here, for each of them speaks for itself and merits careful attention. They are not party policy and they may never become party policy but they do demonstrate the energy and passion for Iain Duncan Smith's agenda from the Conservative rank and file.

But from these themes it is possible to draw some conclusions that constitute a body of principles that can shape our detailed policy work.

The first principle restates the timeless truth that everyone matters. Every individual is important. We explore this principle through the issue of drug dependency but there are many other areas that could have been chosen. We must not tire of telling ourselves that no matter how humble the origin or background, no matter how badly twisted the body or handicapped the brain, no matter what colour the skin or which country of origin, no matter which God you worship or the creed, whether secular or religious, by which you live, the next Conservative Government will govern for you. Everyone knows that the party is for the aspirational, the high-fliers, and the entrepreneurs. That must remain true whilst shifting our focus, our resources and our language behind those less fortunate. Everyone matters.

Next we bring to centre stage the vital principle that all our help should support people – wherever possible – towards achieving independence. In this age of sentimentalism it is easy to overlook that simple truth. We live at a time where so many feel dependent on the state, not just for income but also for problem solving. This has denuded so many of the dignity of discretion, the freedom of standing on our own two feet. The leader of Kent County Council writes powerfully about some of his authority's schemes that are seeking to encourage independence and ensure that no one gets left behind. We are no friend to so many of the vulnerable if our help leaves them languishing in their dependency. But Conservatives must also recognise that through accident of birth or some crushing life blow there are those who need more long term support. Much more work needs to be done on delivery mechanisms, for that support best originates in and through society. Our preference is for locally based, people-sized organisations to take the lead in caring for vulnerable people. The monopolistic and monochrome structures of the state have failed the poor for too long.

In renewing society, the Conservative Party faces some tough choices.

If we are to succeed in making real inroads into some of our major social challenges, we will have to tackle forbidden issues and drive our tanks onto uncharted lawns. Some of the old walls erected in different days must be torn down. Nor should we be constrained by tramlines built along traditional government departmental lines. And so we need a paradigm shift. Some scream 'nanny state' the very instant there is talk about expanding parenting classes. But we must recognise that if new mothers and fathers who themselves have never had stable role models are to provide the boundaries, and encouragement that their own children will need, someone is going to have to teach them basic parenting skills. The Conservative Party needs to be at the forefront of the debate on how to do this – learning from best practice and marshalling the considerable resources and reach of the voluntary, charitable and community-based sector.

We should challenge the long hours culture and celebrate those who seek to put their families first. We must join forces with those who rail against the age discrimination that now cuts absurdly short so many successful careers. We need to bravely confront the debt problems that stalk families and which betray many of our culture's false priorities. We need to embrace policies that take from the able and give to the poor, but always ensuring that this just and proper redistribution is delivered through society – not the state. We have to challenge, not just big government, but also some of the unethical and unhealthy practices of big business if we are to bring about social change. There must be no sacred cows if we are to help vulnerable people in meaningful and sustainable ways.

Equally as important, we have to shift our thinking about government spending from prevention to cure. This will inevitably mean significant up-front investment in order to produce long-term financial and human benefits. We find no difficulty in adopting a 'return on capital invested' formula in the financial world; we must also embrace this simple idea in the social sphere. It may well be that some other stakeholders – not just the taxpayer – have a real pecuniary interest in prevention and can be persuaded to help make the initial investment in exchange for longer-term gains. Insurers, for example, might be persuaded to invest in preventative measures. There has been much talk of joined-up government, under both parties. In truth, I have never seen much evidence of it. Each department concerns itself only with the spending from its own jam jar. We now need a new approach that looks at government spending as a whole, short term and long term.

To get the job done, we have to face up to some tough truths. It would be preferable to live in a world where everyone could live as they pleased and no one gets hurt. But that is not how it is. The commentators and research studies now demonstrate the impact on a young life of a dysfunctional start. All of our instincts are to allow people the freedom to choose how they live, provided they do not harm others. But where there are children involved should we not be encouraging the protection and stability that their young lives so desperately need? The vulnerable suffer disproportionately from an 'anything goes' attitude. We explore the vital need to do more to support the stability that marriage can bring, whilst recognising that other forms of families need first-class support too. It is no good continuing to gather evidence about the development of a life deprived of love and security in the early years but say that it is too difficult to act. We have to act if we are to avoid social disintegration.

The purpose of our book is not to put forward the unremarkable notion that Conservatives care about the poor, but rather that it should be our top priority. We should be passionate in the cause of those left behind, because the cruel waste of human capital offends us. It is an affront to all that we believe about each person achieving his or her potential. We should be outraged at £400 billion spent every year to maintain a system that keeps people dependent and often miserable.

We should also be confident that it is only the Conservative Party that can help the vulnerable because ours is the only party without a vested interest in the system that perpetuates many of the causes of vulnerability.

The media have misunderstood the Conservatives' helping vulnerable people agenda. It is not about extending laissez-faire doctrines throughout society. Conservatives must not stand for social liberalism, but social justice. We must not just represent the small platoons against big government but against big business when it, too, threatens vulnerable people. Our agenda must be the agenda of sustainable compassion and we must eschew politically correct sentimentalism. We must be willing to take on the vested interests of the welfare state if we are to build the welfare society. We must be willing to free the great professions from the dead hand of central control. We must champion the interests of the poor in every part of Britain. Only then will the Conservative Party deserve the people's respect again.

There is such a thing as society

Acknowledgements

My thanks focus on the Conservative Party's Renewing One Nation team. Peter Franklin and Tim Montgomerie within the team have provided much of the vision for *There is such a thing as society* and have worked with and assisted every contributor. I would also like to thank other team members – Kirsten Bird, Jill Kirby, Guy Hordern and Cameron Watt – and my fellow R1N Directors – MPs Oliver Letwin and David Lidington.

Special thanks go to the business leader and philanthropist Sir Stanley Kalms for his generous financial support of the team. He was the first to see the importance of what has become the party's emphasis on 'helping vulnerable people'.

At Politico's Iain Dale has been a wise and patient source of advice. Kreig Barrie's wonderful drawings bring the twelve principles of compassionate conservatism to life. Andrew Burkinshaw's advice on every text was insightful.

Thanks also to Greg Clark, Stephen Crabb, David Godfrey, Robert Halfon, Jonathan Hellewell, Paul McGee, Marvin Olasky, Philippa Stroud, Ruth Steer, Virginia Taylor, Loredana Vuoto, Ron West, Don and Tiffany Willett and Annie Winsbury.

And a final, special thanks to all who wrote the essays that are at the heart of this book. The essays represent only the views of each contributor. This book is not a statement of Conservative party policy. But the essays represent a tremendous contribution to the renewal of the Conservative vision and its relevance to people of every background, colour and creed.

Part one

The challenges

Easterhouse stories

Sandy Weddell

Sandy has been pastor of Easterhouse Baptist Church for 22 years. The church leads or is involved in a number of social action projects. A married father of two, Sandy Weddell was a engineer before he became a minister. Sandy Weddell showed Iain Duncan Smith around the Easterhouse estate in February 2002.

Easterhouse was the solution to a problem. Like all major cities in Britain, Glasgow struggled with the effects of inadequate housing and the rising expectations of a population which had endured the rigours of a second world war. The old one-roomed house affectionately known as 'the single end' was no longer viable and had passed its sell-by date. The people needed to be rehoused and the dreams of many became a reality when Glasgow decided to build four large housing areas or 'schemes' in different outlying parts of the city. On 14 October 1953 the Glasgow Herald newspaper reported: 'Another Township to be known as Easterhouse is proposed for development in the eastern areas.'

The primary housing would be six-in-a-block tenement flats, known in the local language as a 'close'. The sentiments were admirable; solve the problem of slums and the detrimental effects of poverty by giving the people access to good accommodation. Many participants in this transition still talk with great affection about moving from the 'single end' into the kind of housing with an inside toilet and living room separate from the bedrooms. The rent for a four-apartment house was £2:16/8d and the rates £4:19/1d per month, good value, but when one takes into account that the average rent paid by most of the people up to this point was £2:10/-d per quarter, then even at its inception there was a financial struggle to make the ends meet.

It's hard to grasp that around 25,000 to 30,000 people were uprooted and effectively placed out in the country in nice tenement flats without any local shops, cinemas and amenities of any sort. (The lack of the latter is now part of the folk history for the area and is repeated mantra-like in any discussion of the old days). Yet while these were things that people could cope with, there was a more serious underlying problem.

Governing bodies can relocate people, but they cannot relocate a community spirit. The latter flows from relationships, honed from the various interactions of people over many years. My experience of fifties tenement life was one where most families had lived together for successive generations and codes of conduct were passed down through these generational relationships. I knew the boundaries and mores of my community and its expectations of me. When people are relocated through the merging of different communities this 'teaching of the generations' is invariably lost, leaving the new entity struggling for a substitute. In Easterhouse, the community scaffolding was fragile and very quickly both houses and people were shaken by the tremors of a changing society, which was beginning to swing in the sixties. Soon cracks began to appear not just in the plaster of the buildings but also in the fabric of its society. The solution became the problem.

I doubt whether places like Easterhouse have a single story or history, but rather several narratives, reflecting a kaleidoscope of human relationships, fusing together to form the final essay.

The unloved become the unloving

In these places the dominant story reported by the media will be the effects of poverty in its various forms. The problems of unemployment, crime, drugs, debt, lone sharks, family breakdown, single parents, the urban nomads and the general anti-social behaviour. Many participate in this story because of poor life choices, others are press-ganged. It's easy to stand in judgement, yet so often when we scrape the surface we find it is the unloved becoming the unloving, the abused becoming the abuser, the victim becoming the victimiser.

Many years ago in a local school, a chair was suddenly thrown across the classroom. The culprit, a ten-year-old, objected to something a classmate did and after calming the situation I thought nothing more of it until the following week at the school assembly when my little chair-throwing friend began to move towards me with a strange look in his eye. I was stirred but not shaken when he took hold of my hand, looked up and said: 'Mr Weddell, I'm going to see my mum this weekend, she lives in Manchester, I've not seen her for a year.' Call it revelation, insight, whatever it was, that day the little chair-thrower taught me to look beyond the disruption, beyond the pest, beyond the wanting to give him a good shake and see the wee human being struggling with the overwhelming sadness that was called his life.

Yet there is a second narrative and it concerns people who have experienced similar things but have not chosen the self-destructive or anti-social route. Local people and councillors who have worked energetically to create 'the something better than they have'. People refusing to give their streets up to the drug addicts and vandals. Whether it is the ordinary man who decided that what was needed in his area was a credit union and so one began in his house. Or the mothers who really got MAD at the drug dealers in their area and formed Mothers Against Drugs.

Then there is the third story of the 'professionals'. Teachers who choose to remain rather than go to a 'better school', social workers, policemen and women, community workers who do more than a job, it's the story of professionals, determined to go the extra mile. Within this narrative the Church, manifested in its different denominations, is terminally committed through its members and projects. Three years ago our own church, through the experience of observing children eating the leftovers of the communion bread, realised that many of them were beginning the day hungry. We started a breakfast club that not only ensures children go to school with something in their stomachs but also have a secure and stable base to begin the day from.

The fourth story is the sometimes tense relationship between Government structures and local aspirations. A vast amount of work is done through these agencies with the community benefiting from the tireless work done by many individuals. Yet for all the good work being accomplished the perception still exists, among many on the ground, that there is 'a them and us', with the agencies controlling the purse strings and ultimately the agenda. Whether this is simply a difference in personalities, a difficulty of communication with the faults lying on both sides, or pointing to the deeper problem concerning the redistribution of power is open for debate. Whatever approach we prefer we have to acknowledge that this tension exists and has to be resolved.

Iain Duncan Smith and Easterhouse

An unexpected turn in my experience of the story of Easterhouse came on 2 February 2002 when I found myself welcoming Ian Duncan Smith to the area. I required a reformatting and rebooting of my internal presuppositions because I never saw the Tories as being anything other than a footnote in the history of the place.

Like others who met with Mr Duncan Smith I was impressed by him; especially refreshing was to hear a politician seeking to understand a problem before giving an answer to it. I do believe that he is genuine in his attempt to wrestle with some of the problems that Easterhouse and similar situations present for the Conservative Party.

In his challenging book *Faith in the Poor* Bob Holman allows us an insight into some of the economic hardships ordinary people in Easterhouse face. A One Nation Conservative Party must dialogue with people who literally have to count their pennies because pennies are all they have. Then there are the faith communities, who are happy to serve the poor but not the secular presuppositions of governing bodies. A few weeks ago at a meeting with fellow ministers for the area I was saddened when I heard how one church, seeking to take about thirty kids off the streets on behalf of a local football team, was refused a grant, because it was a church. How is the Conservative Party going to relate to faith communities? They must be one of the most underused resources in deprived areas.

Another challenge is ensuring that government agencies not only meet targets but embrace a community servanthood which is willing to have faith (usually spelt R I S K) in local social entrepreneurship and whose mission statement reads: 'They must increase and we must decrease.' Or in the language of this essay: how can we ensure that these agencies are incorporated into the second and third narratives rather than the other way round?

The final chapter is still to be written in the story that is Easterhouse, and hopefully it will have a happy ending. The 'close' is going the same way as the 'single end', being replaced by modern centrally heated housing. The dreams of many are becoming a reality and many talk about finding solutions to the problem, but the cracks are still there.

Sunil, Sarah and Michael: Growing up in Britain

John Glen and Hannah Parker

John Glen has been a management consultant with Accenture for five years and is currently studying for an MBA in Cambridge. He is a trustee of a national youth charity and a former school governor in Lewisham. John was the Conservative candidate for Plymouth Devonport in 2001.

Hannah Parker is National Chairman of Conservative Future, a post she has been elected to and held for two years running. She currently works in human resources at the Financial Times. She is also a school governor, has nursed in India, studied in the USA, and worked on a water project in Uganda and with the homeless in the UK.

Young people from around the world believe that the UK has an excellent higher education system and is good at business, they also accept that we have a democratic

society and efficient institutions. But they are critical of
our social relationships and in general young people
around the world respect us more than they like us. They
have a positive image of the UK as a country but are less
admiring of us Britons as a people.[1]

How often do we recognise the reality of who we are as a nation?
Whilst Britain is an affluent society by many definitions it is
wrong to say that this wealth and well-being is the universal
experience of all its people.

This chapter tells the story of three young people and their
experience of growing up in Britain. Although Sunil, Sarah and
Michael are fictional devices for the purpose of this essay their
experiences are an accurate reflection of the reality of daily life
for many young people.

Sunil's story

Sunil (aged seven) is a second-generation Ugandan Asian from
the West Midlands. His parents were among the 27,000 Ugandan
Asian immigrants admitted to the UK in 1972.[2] They have done
well building up their own small business importing specialist
clothing from Mumbai. Sunil's grandparents, who live with his
family, do not speak any English and the language spoken at home
is Hindi. Sunil's family own a semi-detached house with a
mortgage (along with 57 per cent of families with Indian origins
compared to the national average of 42 per cent).[3] Sunil sees
himself as very fortunate as there are 13,700 homeless households

19

in the West Midlands – the second highest rate outside London.[4] He is a pupil at the same local primary school that his brothers attended, the eldest of whom, Ravi, has, like sixty per cent of students of Indian origin, gained more than five GCSEs (A–C), which is the best performance of any ethnic group in Britain and rather more than the national average of 49 per cent.[5] Ravi is also more likely to graduate than children from any other background.[6] Twenty-nine per cent of Sunil's classes have more than 31 pupils,[7] against the optimal class size of 20–25 pupils.[8]

Sadly, Sunil's best friend Simon has been having a hard time recently. Last year, along with 10,099 others, he was added to the child protection register for neglect (twenty per cent more than were added in 1997).[9] The main reason for this was because Simon burnt himself badly when left alone at home. His grandmother had been due to look after him but was unexpectedly taken ill and so Simon was left unsupervised. Simon is also on free school meals, which means that he is statistically more likely to be excluded from school.[10]

When not at school Sunil and Simon love to play football, just like 62 per cent of boys of their age group.[11] But Sunil has recently been diagnosed with asthma. This is the first incidence of this condition in his family, but Sunil has become one of 13.2 per cent of boys[12] from his age group to suffer with this condition. Data combining new diagnoses of asthma with new attacks shows that the incidence is six times higher in children than it was 25 years ago.[13] Despite always enjoying a wide and diverse group of friends Sunil was recently attacked by older boys from the local senior school. It was thought to be racially motivated. Over 56 per cent of school pupils have been victims of crime in 2001; 71 per cent of these are committed by other young people.[14]

Sarah's story

Sarah lives with her mother in a council house in the North East. Sarah was born the youngest of three children into a home where money had always been tight. The average GDP per head in the region is the lowest in the country at 77 per cent of the UK's average.[15] Her father, Sam, was a miner. After twenty years in the job Sam retrained in the mid-1980s, but never fully adjusted to employment outside the industry. Sarah cannot remember a time when her father held a steady job; she grew up as one of twenty per cent of children who live in a household where no-one works.[16] Sam was diagnosed with rheumatoid arthritis in 1991. He signed on to incapacity benefit and became one of 3.1 million others to receive sick and/or disabled benefits in 2001.[17] Sarah became one of 2.7 million children growing up in a household that depends on Income Support or Jobseeker's Allowance as a source of income.[18] Sarah's father was also prone to bouts of depression and her mother became dependent on alcohol, along with four per cent of the UK population.[19] The marriage broke down and Sarah's father left the family home, they finally divorced in 1999, one of 159,000 couples who did so that year;[20] this compares to 74,000 who divorced in 1971.[21] As part of a lone-parent household Sarah joined three times as many similar children than existed in 1963.[22]

There is such a thing as society

Sarah could not cope with the new home environment and ran away for the first time, as do 77,000 other children each year. She was just twelve years old but older than some – one in four first-time runaways are under eleven years old.[23] During her month away she slept rough, as do 34 per cent of runaways, and it was during this period that Sarah become part of the 8.3 per cent of her age who take drugs.[24] Soon after the police brought Sarah home she was put into local authority care where 58,100 other children are looked after.[25] Thirty-eight per cent of young prisoners have at some point been taken into local authority care before the age of sixteen.[26] It was at this point that Sarah's mother reached rock bottom and became one of the 28,000 annual hospital admissions for alcohol dependence.[27]

After eight months in care Sarah returned to her mother but the relationship between them was strained. Life was made even harder by the fact that Sarah had moved home and therefore to a new school where she had no friends. Sarah had never been a high achiever, but she did not settle at her new school and became one of the 26 per cent of girls who fail to reach the expected level at Key Stage 3.[28] Following a common pattern for former runaways[29] she started being bullied and, as with so many young people, she felt unable to talk to her parents about it. Instead, she became one of the 22,372 children who call Childline about bullying every year.[30] Despite her school's best efforts to address Sarah's difficulties Sarah found the stress of school life too much. She started playing truant, as 50,000 children do every school day in the UK,[31] and hanging out with older boys in town. Sarah's days were filled with little constructive activity. She started drinking, joining one of the 31 per cent of fourteen-year-old girls who regularly consume alcohol.[32] And like twelve per cent of her age group[33] she started smoking cannabis.

Amongst her group of friends was Dave, a nineteen-year-old unemployed man who was on probation for drug offences. Dave seemed very attentive to Sarah and within a few weeks they started a sexual relationship. Unfortunately, Dave was one of the 47 per cent of sixteen-to-nineteen-year-old men who do not use a condom[34] and Sarah became pregnant at fifteen (one of the 4.5 per cent in the fifteen-to-seventeen age group who fall pregnant each year).[35] As soon as Dave found out about the baby he decided not to see Sarah any more. Sarah didn't feel she could tell her Mum but tried to talk to the few girlfriends she had. All advised her to have an abortion. However, Sarah decided not to be one of the 600 women who have an abortion every working day (183,250 in total during 1999).[36] Nine months later, two days before her sixteenth birthday Sarah gave birth to Jimmy. She became one of almost ninety per cent of mothers under twenty who give birth to babies outside marriage. Of the same group, 27 per cent have no father's name on the birth certificate.[37] Unusually, Sarah decided to give Jimmy up for adoption (there were 8,000 children adopted in 1992, compared to 27,000 in 1968).[38]

Sarah formally left school the next week with no qualifications along with 75 per cent of children who have been in care.[39]

There is such a thing as society

Michael's story

Michael is sixteen years old and until recently he lived with both his parents in a large detached house on the outskirts of Manchester. Michael's parents both enjoy successful careers. His father is the managing director of a successful business in Manchester but is frequently away on business. Michael's mother is equally busy – having carved out a successful career at the Bar. She is one of 65 per cent of mothers with children under eighteen who work full or part time.[40] She is often at home but didn't see much of Michael as he spent a lot of time watching television in line with the average Briton, who watches 19 hours and 52 minutes of television every week (21.3 per cent of leisure time).[41] The family rarely ate together – again reflecting the national trend.

Michael went to a good local school but despite great parental expectations he did not perform well due to belatedly recognised learning difficulties. Michael struggled in his GCSE classes and his teachers did not think it likely that he would gain the required grades for A-level study. Michael is prone to despondency and does not enjoy a good relationship with his parents, who never properly acknowledged the challenges he faced at school. Whilst 83 per cent of adults say it is very important to listen to children and young people only 57 per cent agree that they do listen.[42] Michael certainly feels that his parents did not listen to him.

Michael was one of the in crowd at his school, and regularly smoked a quick joint during break times. After he was caught rolling a spliff by the Deputy Head – for the second time – he was instantly expelled. He was immediately put in the local sixth form college's intensive GCSE revision class by his parents, who hoped this might help him with his grades. It did not and he began spending time with other pupils who thought working for exams was a waste of time.

One of his new friends explained how mobile phones could be cloned. Michael owned the latest model, which he knew his father would quickly replace if 'lost', so he handed this over for the extra cash. Having the increased money in his pockets led Michael to start stealing mobile phones from schoolmates. This developed into theft from members of the public. Sixty per cent of crimes committed by excluded pupils involve the handling of stolen goods.[43] One day, after grabbing a phone from another youth, a fight developed in which Michael's victim was injured. Michael was arrested. A switchblade knife was found on him and he was charged for grievous bodily harm and put on remand – becoming one of 2,370 young people (defined as fifteen-to-twenty-year-olds) in March 2002.[44] He was subsequently sentenced for violence against the person[45] and became one of the sixteen per cent of the total 69,780 prison population that is aged between fifteen and twenty[46] and one of 1,670 young men convicted for violence against the person.[47] Since beginning his six-month sentence Michael has had the opportunity to exercise for one hour a day with the remaining time spent on C Block with more experienced offenders. He is living what the experts report, that 'purposeful activity has increased for each prisoner by just ten minutes a day in ten years'.[48]

Conclusion

When we read stories of deprivation, hardship and suffering we hope they're only true of a few isolated instances. Very often this is simply not true. Despite the undoubted prosperity of our times, the experiences of Sunil, Sarah and Michael are representative of many young people. In a relatively brief overview we cannot hope to cover every relevant issue. Instead, these stories are intended as a snapshot of life for some of Britain's children in 2002. It is a challenge to everyone concerned about the young people we share this island with. This book is a considered attempt to respond to their needs and hopes.

1   British Council, 'Through other eyes 2: How the world sees the United Kingdom', 2001/02

2   www.britkid.org, 'Timeline of Ethnic Minorities in Britain'

3   Office of National Statistics, *Social Trends 2002*, tables 10.9 and 10.11, page 168/9

4   Office of National Statistics, *Social Trends 2002*, table 10.12, page 169

5   Office of National Statistics, *Social Trends 2002*, table 3.16, page 62

6   Office of National Statistics, *Social Trends 2002*, table 3.17, page 62

7   Office of National Statistics, *Social Trends 2002*, table 3.4, page 55

8   Office of National Statistics, *Social Trends 2002*, page 56

9   NSPCC, *Child Neglect 2002*

10 Office of National Statistics, *Social Trends 2002*, page 21

11 Office of National Statistics, *Social Trends 2002*, page 23

12 Office of National Statistics, *Social Trends 2002*, page 21

13 Office of National Statistics, *Social Trends 2002*, page 21; National Asthma Campaign Asthma Audit 2001

14 MORI, 2002 Youth Survey

15 Office of National Statistics, *Social Trends 2002*, table 5.27, page 104

16 NCH, Annual Review 2000/1, page 9

John Glen and Hannah Parker

17   Office of National Statistics, *Social Trends 2002*, table 8.17, page 144

18   NCH, Annual Review 2000/1, page 9

19   www.think-net.org, 'Alcohol – have we got it under control?', July 2002

20   Office of National Statistics, *Social Trends 2002*, page 44

21   www.bbc.co.uk/news, 'Divorce rate lowest for 22 years', 21 August 2001

22   Office of National Statistics, *Social Trends 2002*, page 41

23   The Children's Society, *Child Runaways*, November 1999

24   www.bbc.co.uk, Drugs Special Report

25   NSPCC *Summary of Child Protection Register Statistics*, 2001

26   National Prison Survey 1991, quoted in a Written Parliamentary Answer by Beverley
      Hughes, *Hansard*, column 324W, 24 April 2002

27   www.think-net.org, Alcohol – have we got it under control?, July 2001

28   Office of National Statistics, *Social Trends 2002*, table 3.15, page 61

29   The Children's Society, 'Child Runaways', November 1999

30   Office of National Statistics, *Social Trends 2002*, table 8.21, page 146

31   *Guardian Schools*, 'Two day sentences for parents of truants', 12 July 2002

32   Office of National Statistics, *Social Trends 2002*, table 7.16, page 128

33   Office of National Statistics, *Social Trends 2002*, page 129

34   Office of National Statistics, *Social Trends 2002*, table 7.26, page 133

35   Office of National Statistics, *Social Trends 2002*, page 22

36   *'Responding to the Culture of Death – A Primer of Bioethical Issues'*, Day One
      Publications, 2001, page 31

37   Office of National Statistics, *Social Trends 2002*, page 47

38   *Responding to the Culture of Death – A Primer of Bioethical Issues*, Day One
      Publications, 2001, page 31

39   NCH, Annual Review 2000/01, page 15

40   Office of National Statistics, *Social Trends 2002*, page 19

41   BBC, Annual Report 2002

42   Childline, 'Are young people being heard', March/April 2002

43   Mori, 2002 Youth Survey, May 2002

44   Home Office, *Prison Population*, March 2002, summary

45   Home Office, *Prison Population*, March 2002, page 13, table 1

46   Home Office, *Prison Population*, March 2002, page 12

47   Home Office, *Prison Population*, March 2002, page 13

48   Juliet Lyon, *Guardian*, 'Last Resort', 19 May 2002

Part two

The Conservative response

The renewal of society

Iain Duncan Smith

Iain Duncan Smith is Leader of the Conservative Party and Member of Parliament for Chingford and Woodford Green. Iain is a trustee of Whitefields Development Trust, a special needs school and is a patron of Haven House, a children's hospice charity in his constituency. He is married to Betsy with four school age children.

It was once said that you need a dream to get up in the morning. I believe that a renewal of idealism is urgently needed to restore enthusiasm for British politics.

Idealism was once much stronger. Great causes such as freedom, racial justice and compassion for the poor energised public life. But enthusiasm for great causes has drained away as the methods used to pursue them have failed.

The sense of disillusionment is particularly deep today because of the manner of Labour's failure. Hopes were high in 1997 when Tony Blair was elected with a massive majority, the most favourable of economic climates; and the expectant goodwill of the people. But after more than five years of spin and hype people feel badly let down. Young people, in particular, are turning away from a Government that favours managerialism over mission and presentation over purpose. Cynical politics breeds popular cynicism about politics and so the cycle continues.

Disillusion is most profound amongst those in greatest need. Many people on Britain's poorest housing estates have come to despair at ever seeing life improve. But from within these same estates come possible solutions. It is therefore fitting that this book should open with a foreword from Sandy Weddell. Sandy is the minister of the Easterhouse Baptist Church. Easterhouse is one of the largest and most hard-pressed housing estates in Europe. In February, Sandy showed me around the estate and I saw for myself the problems of that deeply disadvantaged – but still resolute – community. A few weeks later I said to delegates at the Conservative Spring Conference:

> It's not just about winning votes for the Conservative Party in places like Easterhouse. It's about meaning what we say: that there are no 'no-go' areas as far as we are concerned. It's about being a Party that doesn't just drive past Easterhouse on the motorway.' I concluded that speech with these words: 'A nation that leaves its vulnerable behind, diminishes its own future. Britain will never be all that it should be until opportunity and security mean something to people in Easterhouse. To make this country theirs as much as it is ours. That is a mission fit for a new century.

There is such a thing as society

It is a mission that I have accepted on behalf of the Conservative Party and it will define what we think, say and do from this present time of policy renewal, through to the electoral battles ahead of us and then on into government.

It is time to outline key principles that will give shape, form and colour to our mission. This book should not be read as a statement of official policy. Instead it should be seen as the latest response of free-thinking Conservatives to the social challenges that have defeated a tax-and-spend Labour party that has turned its back on new thinking. This book represents the commitment of Conservatives to fresh thinking but thinking founded on a distinctively Conservative approach. Some of our ideals are shared by our political opponents but we are unburdened by their slavish devotion to outdated methods. Conservatives are breaking out of stale left-versus-right, state-versus-market arguments. There are new faultlines in British politics. The Labour and Conservative parties are champions of increasingly different worldviews. Labour champions centralism against localism; uniformity above diversity; control instead of innovation; bureaucracy rather than democracy. Most of all it is the state–society faultline that is central to the divide between Tony Blair and myself.

Renewal not reinvention

Margaret Thatcher's now famous words about society were, of course, wrenched from their context and grotesquely misrepresented. She knew that people naturally provide each other with mutual support. They start families, build businesses, help charities and even join political parties. The governments she led encouraged the free decisions by which free people build society. The way that certain commentators reported Margaret Thatcher's remarks was used to mischaracterise what the Conservatives stood for. To some extent, Conservatives still face the same mistrust. The general welcome to the focus on helping vulnerable people has been tempered with the desire for more evidence that I mean what I say. Part of the evidence is in this book and in the lives of its contributors – the thinkers and the doers that prove that Conservatives have always cared about vulnerable people. For we need to be clear that the Conservative Party is not reinventing itself, but rediscovering and renewing an historic identity shaped by the caring hearts and practical agendas of Burke and Disraeli, Wilberforce and Shaftesbury, Salisbury and Churchill, Macleod and Joseph.

But this begs the question: why the need for renewal? The answer lies in the great twentieth-century battle between socialism and free market democracy. From our twenty-first-century perspective we sometimes forget the degree to which politics was defined by this struggle. Throughout it all, it fell to the Conservatives to stand against two perilous threats to our freedom: firstly, the idea that the collective is of greater worth than the person; and secondly, the idea that the planned economy was more efficient and fair than the free market. It was a fight that came to a climax in the 1980s. It was a fight we won.

Shared success

Most people don't live to work, they work to live – if, that is, work is available at all. So while the Conservative mission must continue to enable people to fulfil their aspirations we must have a broader understanding of what that means. We all dream dreams, we all have ambitions, we all want success – but that doesn't just take place in a world of aggressive, go-getting, upwardly mobile individual achievement. Success at paid work is not all that counts. It is not what people do but what they are that matters. It is our values – not our income or wealth – that define each of us.

Outside of work people can and do succeed but, more often than not, their successes are shared successes. A shared success can take on many forms. A closely-knit family will bring generations together and build character and identity. Following or being part of a local sports team creates community. Giving time to a charity can be a transforming experience for both the giver and 'beneficiary'. There is nothing trivial, passive or vicarious in sharing success. Shared achievement is often the most noble and inspiring enterprise that anyone can be involved in because it requires the sacrifice of individual priorities. The institutions in which we share success – families, communities, charities – often provide us with material security but also with a sense of identity and belonging that neither the market nor the state can provide. The Chief Rabbi, Dr Jonathan Sacks, calls them covenantal institutions. These covenantal institutions – these sources of shared success and identity – are particularly important for people at certain stages of life and during difficult times. Children and very old people, in particular, depend upon them. When people are hit by life shocks such as unemployment, bereavement or sickness it is these institutions that often hold people together. We will only tackle the deepest manifestations of poverty and alienation when we rebuild the people-sized institutions of free society.

The Conservative alternative

If Conservatives are to build on our past, we must also learn from Labour's current mistakes. Labour's most serious error is its failure to understand how society works. They got into power by characterising the Conservative Party as only about individualism and materialism. They were wrong and that has meant that they have gone back to centralisation, as a false alternative. This is a Government that believes that it can only deliver through structures that are imposed on people, not composed of them. However much Labour really wants to reform the public services it will not succeed because it relies on impersonal bureaucracies entirely unsuited to the very personal situations in which vulnerable people find themselves. New Labour's obsession with auditing, targets and indicators means that if it can't be counted, then it doesn't count. The conclusion of this mechanistic view of man's worth is to reason that professional pride doesn't count, that the voluntary spirit doesn't count, that personal compassion doesn't count.

Conservatives understand that shared success is important to everyone, but especially to many vulnerable people for whom individual achievement is less easily secured. The Conservative Party must be the party of aspiration for everyone. That means assisting people to take part in the shared successes of family, community and nation. We understand that taking part involves an element of personal sacrifice but governments must also learn to make sacrifices. The next Conservative Government will play its part by sacrificing power, handing it over to the people that are in a better position to use it effectively: doctors, nurses and patients; teachers, pupils and parents; police officers, volunteers and good neighbours.

Labour have failed the British people's ideals by politicising and centralising welfare and the public services. They have disappointed through incompetence and disillusioned by raising and then blighting the hopes of communities across Britain.

Over eighteen years in office Conservatives directed the resources of government towards the creation of an environment that fostered economic entrepreneurship. The next Conservative Government must direct its energies to a parallel project: the encouragement of social entrepreneurship and support for the people-sized institutions of society. The extraordinary character of everyday service is the only sure foundation of a socially just society. Every citizen has a part to play. The son caring for his elderly and sick mother. The neighbour visiting a housebound invalid. The teacher running an after-school arts club. The police officer patrolling and reassuring a neighbourhood. The small businessman working tirelessly to provide a little extra for his family. Over many years the centralised state has tended to replace rather than renew these forms of service. They have been scorned by politicians who impose simplistic blueprints on a complex and dynamic society. The time has come to recognise these people as each community's heroes.

Government must become the servant of society – not its master. Government's proper role lies in actively sustaining healthy family networks, active citizenship and professional freedom. Labour's failed methods must not kill idealism. The task for Conservatives is to dig deep into the one nation heritage of our party. Our aim must be to provide a fresh environment in which great causes can breathe and prosper. It is time to liberate the nation's ideals from Labour's suffocating embrace. That begins with the renewal of society.

For Labour there is no such thing as society, only the state

Oliver Letwin

Oliver Letwin is Shadow Home Secretary and MP for Dorset West. Oliver is a director of Renewing One Nation and was previously a member of the Prime Minister's Policy Unit (1983-86). Married with two children he is author of Ethics, Emotion and the Unity of the Self *(1984),* Aims of Schooling *(1988),* Drift to Union *(1990),* The Purpose of Politics *(1999) and* Beyond the Causes of Crime *(2002).*

Sustainability and the state

Society has been a difficult word for Conservatives in recent times. In a grotesquely misrepresented interview in 1987 Margaret Thatcher said:

> We've been through a period where too many people have been given to understand that if they have a

problem, it's the government's job to cope with it. 'I have a problem, I'll get a grant'. 'I'm homeless, the government must house me.' They're casting their problems on society. And you know, there's no such thing as society. There are individual men and women, there are families. And no government can do anything except through people, and people must look after themselves first. It's our duty to look after ourselves and then, also, to look after our neighbours.[1]

Mrs Thatcher was attacking the Left's unthinking call for 'society' to rush in and solve every ill. And when the Left say 'society' – then and still today – they inevitably mean the state. In the part of the quotation that the Left never repeat, Mrs Thatcher points to a more enduring vision of society – a society composed of active citizens and strong families.

This book and its twelve principles set out to renew this Conservative vision of society. Conservatives believe that society flourishes on a human scale – in hugely varied people-sized institutions that are connected by a complex web of mutually enriching relationships. The institutions and relationships of society provide each of us with a sense of identity and belonging. They are multidimensional in purpose. They have evolved organically and have stood the test of time.

Conservatives believe that the main role of government is to support the institutions of society and the complex, infinitely varied relationships between them. The state's role should never be to supplant or nationalise society. This state–society distinction is absent from Labour's worldview. It is true to say that for New Labour there is no such thing as society, only the state.

Free enterprise and the state

Before the Thatcher Governments the state interfered in every nook and cranny of economic life. Whenever the state suppressed the price mechanism – as British Governments often did before 1979 – they blocked out the information that is the basis of a properly functioning economy. Through heavy taxation and regulation, the same Governments supplanted the entrepreneurs and small businesses who ensure that consumers' infinitely varied demands are heard and heeded. In ignoring the complexity of relations between market players the state produced the catastrophic economic mess of the 1970s.

That was the reality that faced the Conservative Government elected in May 1979. It began a programme of bold reforms that freed people to make their own economic decisions. That Conservative Government trusted entrepreneurs, businesses, and trade union members to make economic decisions instead of politicians, monopolies and union barons.

Under Conservatives the state's vital role was limited to creating and then maintaining a hospitable environment for free enterprise. The market was naturally self-sustaining if protected from external shocks and the sometimes dangerous tendencies of producers to adopt monopolistic practices. That is why Conservative Governments of the 1980s waged war on inflation, renewed competition policy, liberalised the financial sector and reduced high marginal rates of tax.

Today the Conservative focus is different but similar philosophical issues are at stake. Our belief is that Labour's expansion of the centralised state threatens society as much today as it once threatened free enterprise. Government must undertake a fundamental redirection of its energies. It must transform itself to become the servant and protector of society's institutions and relationships.

The essays in this book show the coherence of the Conservative message and the fundamental importance we attach to the three major themes of high-quality public services, localisation and effective compassion for disadvantaged people.

Sustainability and the natural environment

There are, I believe, four key warnings from environmental science's understanding of the damage done to freely evolved systems by crude human interventions:

1   The real world is irreducibly complex.
2   Simplistic targets can be exceptionally destructive.
3   Crude intervention damages natural regeneration.
4   Systems can absorb a limited amount of disruption before suddenly deteriorating irreversibly.

Firstly, the real world is irreducibly complex. When people work against the grain of nature it is because they think they know nature backwards. They interfere with natural systems confident that they can predict all the consequences of doing so. It's as if they could reduce nature to a simplified model governed by a few ground rules to be manipulated at will, just as socialist governments thought they could do the same with the economy. But increasingly scientists realise that natural systems are irreducibly complex and that we can never reliably predict the consequence of human intervention. For instance, because scientists have mapped out the human genome many people imagine that we now have a working model of what our genes do. But that assumes that there is one function for every gene, and one gene for every function. With 30,000 genes that seems quite complicated enough. The truth is that our genes interact with one another in countless different combinations for countless different functions. This is irreducible complexity that we are only beginning to understand. So while we can start modifying DNA, putting in a gene here, taking one out there – we have no way of being sure of all the consequences. But if the human genome is complicated, what about human society? In this country alone it consists of sixty million elements called human beings – all relating to others in multidimensional ways. Yet while we express concerns about modifying so much as a tomato, the state thinks it can change human nature. Perhaps we should be at least as concerned about social engineering as we are about genetic engineering.

Secondly, simplistic targets can be exceptionally destructive. In 1958 Mao's communists launched the Great Leap Forward that included the 'War Against the Four Pests'. Chief among the

pests was the sparrow, which Mao wanted wiped out. The authorities ordered China's peasants to kill the birds by all available
means – principally by scaring them so that they would drop from
the skies, dead from exhaustion. It 'worked' insofar as millions of
sparrows were killed. And that year China did record a bumper
harvest. But while sparrows eat some grain, they also eat insects.
The next year northern China experienced an unprecedented
plague of locusts that stripped the fields bare. Between 1959 and
1961 over thirty million people starved to death as a result of the
centralising arrogance of the Great Leap Forward. This is an
extreme example of what happens when we intervene in an irreducibly complex system. But that doesn't mean that top-down
targets can't kill – even in Britain. By targeting waiting lists for
hospital operations, without distinguishing between minor
ailments and serious conditions, it is likely that Government
policy has resulted in the loss of life. A target is no substitute for
the judgement of those who shoulder responsibility for others, be
they doctors, nurses, teachers or parents.

Thirdly, crude intervention damages natural regeneration.
Tropical rainforest is the richest habitat on Earth. The biomass
produced per acre of forest greatly exceeds anything that human
agriculture can achieve. But it is not the 'right' kind of biomass,
so it was assumed that we could do better by planting crops on
what was thought to be very rich soil. But tropical rainforests
tend to grow on poor soil. The incredible diversity of the system
is maintained by the diversity itself – by a complex web of interactions between different species that recycles the limited

amounts of nutrients available. Replacing the complexity of the forest with the monoculture of crops reduces once fertile land to little more than desert. In our own society we speak of the importance of diversity, but we have progressively destroyed it. No one would deny that family relationships are complicated. By weakening bonds within the extended family and then within the nuclear family, we may have thought we would make life simpler. But in breaking these links we have made our neighbourhoods less stable and poorer places to raise children. Thus, in many places, we are failing to pass on the values of a neighbourly society to the new generation.

Fourthly, there are 'tipping points'. Systems can absorb a limited amount of disruption before suddenly deteriorating irreversibly. When, for example, trees are cleared from hillsides the result is sometimes soil erosion – an effect which begins almost immediately and progresses gradually. But this is not always the case. Sometimes we think we can get away with destroying the self-sustaining features of a natural environment. Either there is no erosion or it appears manageable. But then we reach a 'tipping point' where the ground becomes soaked with water and a landslide results. In the Himalayas whole villages have been wiped out in this way. And one tipping point can trigger others. With Himalayan mountains denuded of trees and soil, monsoon rains result in flash floods that can kill thousands of people downstream in Bangladesh.

Local, holistic and infinitely varied institutions of society should be the starting point of public policy. Only these institutions – such as the great professions and covenantal institutions like the family – can understand and manage the complexity of the social challenges we face. Government still has the vital role of supporting and protecting society – not least from the excesses of the market economy. But that is not the role Labour has given the state. Labour has invested all of its energies in massive centralised control of health, education and other public services. Such an approach is unsustainable.

Centralised approaches to public service reform are unsustainable

Huge, centralised bureaucracies are unable to handle the complexity of life and information in society. They lack the subtlety to respond to the infinitely varied needs of patients and pupils. They increasingly undermine the independence and judgement of highly qualified professionals.

When centralised schemes fail it takes a long time for Whitehall to notice. Information about results travels slowly up the chain of command. Messages are often confused because a programme can appear to work well – at least for a time – in some localities. When it is increasingly obvious that a programme is failing politicians often take great steps to hide the fact. Whereas a private company would cut its losses and divert resources into profitable projects, a politician will often redouble the effort to make a signature initiative work. This may lead to the diversion of even more resources to the initial misplaced scheme and still greater centralisation.

There is such a thing as society

A vicious circle of intervention is underway. The failure to deliver is unfairly blamed on already disempowered professions and local structures. Desperate bureaucrats shout their orders more loudly at nurses, doctors, teachers and police officers. Patients, parents and victims of crime wonder if they will ever receive better public services.

Conservatives will trust the people

The Conservative response is to decentralise – or localise – power. Conservatives trust people and that means trusting doctors to treat patients, teachers to educate pupils and police officers to catch criminals. Every professional has a natural enthusiasm for their vocation and a strong commitment to serve. Many leave their training college or university with hope and expectation but find these qualities suffocated by the dead hand of central control. Their professionalism is neither trusted nor respected. They are ordered about by a remote bureaucratic apparatus that impatiently pursues artificial targets and is ignorant of local needs. That is why Conservatives pair respect for professionalism with local forms of accountability.

The Conservative approach will ensure patterns of accountability operate on a human scale. Real accountability means less central control and stronger relationships between service providers and the people who depend upon those services. When doctors, nurses, teachers and police officers are rooted in local communities they are best placed to understand and manage those diverse communities' needs. The local community is in the best position to hold them responsible for results but currently lacks opportunities to exercise any real influence.

Localisation creates space for relationships to flourish because it reduces the distance between public service providers and the people intended to benefit from them. Localisation gives parents, patients and local people the opportunity to be involved in shaping the way local services are run. Localisation gives professions the opportunity to develop relations with each other. GPs in one medical centre in the Midlands – appreciating the links between crime and poor health – have invited police officers into their surgery to regularly listen to patients' experiences of crime and for there to be an exchange of intelligence and crime prevention advice. Localisation also establishes far more effective mechanisms for correcting failure because good relations between service providers and the community ensure a ready interchange of information.

A Rowntree report on hard-pressed housing estates identified the localisation of public services as vital for neighbourhood renewal.[2] An active and visible police presence on one particular estate has laid the foundation for a wider improvement in public services – delivered by caretakers who, based in the locality, can provide an immediate response to a broken lift or a badly lit walkway. The author of the Rowntree report identified service level improvements as a 'tipping point issue' for many families deciding whether or not to remain on an increasingly disadvantaged estate.

In Birmingham, neighbourhood wardens regularly escort councillors and public service officials around Balsall Heath. The wardens point out an accident trouble-spot or the youth club's leaking roof. And they point these things out again – if necessary – on the next escorted tour. Action rates have improved dramatically since this face-to-face form of accountability replaced an often unanswered flow of letters.

Centralised, unsustainable policy hurts the poor most

Britain's poorest estates vividly illustrate the destination of centralising tendencies. No communities have become more dependent upon the state than many of our country's most deprived inner-city and peripheral housing estates. Many of them have gone over 'tipping points' into serious lawlessness and environmental degradation. The weakness of societal links and the retreat of a police presence has left them vulnerable to malign gang cultures.

Shiny new buildings may be built and a little more cash fill people's pockets when – through centralised allocations of public money and bureaucratic intervention – the state forces its way into a hard-pressed community. But because this type of intervention does nothing to rebuild the self-sustaining relationships within the community the products of interventions are easily reversed.

But, sadly, it's much worse than that. Interventions by the centralised state often undermine multidimensional relationships. They can also distort a community's sense of values by seeming to reward unsustainable behaviour. Welfare pioneers avoiding doing anything that would damage the bonds between people in need and their families and communities. These bonds were recognised as more durable than help from an 'outside' private or public benefactor. Sometimes these bonds were weak – and sometimes even malign – but they needed to be restored or mended – rather than disregarded. At their best, these bonds represented holistic – or 3D – care. One-dimensional state benefits can compensate for the breadwinning role of an absent father but the state cannot also be a role model for the child or a source of emotional support and care for the child's mother.

Only the renewal of community institutions offers vulnerable people a sustainable possibility of escaping from cycles of deprivation. The National Federation of Community Organisations has noted how community life had been damaged by 'wildly fluctuating housing policies, successive waves of area based regeneration programmes, the growth of single person households [and] changing work patterns'.[3] One member of a London Community Association said: 'We are in a culture which increasingly moves people away from community values . . . What you end up with is lonely people, violence, danger, fear.' This quote illustrates the capacity for survival of the NFCO's 4,000 membership organisations:

> Many associations began several decades ago and over the years they have quietly carried on their work, weathering the changes in priority and cuts in funding of successive Governments, to emerge as a strong network and a stable, mature force for change in the 21st century.

There is such a thing as society

The enormous possible contribution of community organisations and a thousand and one other local people-sized projects has been ignored for too long.

Society is the basis of sustainability

In his Leader's speech to the Scottish Party Conference Iain Duncan Smith got to the heart of this state–society distinction between the Labour and Conservative parties. 'While Labour trusts the state, Conservatives trust people,' he said. 'When Labour thinks of community it thinks of politicians, committees and taskforces. When Conservatives think of community we think of the family, local schools, charities, and places of worship.'[4]

The communities referred to by Iain include a wider society – a society that encompasses the professions, trade unions and universities. These are associations and institutions that flourish when they enjoy independence from the state. Society is characterised by an intricate web of professional, voluntary and involuntary relationships. Professional relationships like a GP's relationship with his or her patients. Voluntary relationships like a mentor's care of an at-risk youth. And then involuntary – or covenantal – relationships like a mother's love for her son.

Society – and the relationships that hold society together – can be sustained by the state or they can be ignored and undermined by the state.

To sustain means to support from below. That is the Conservative vision: government helping to sustain a society that is a rich tapestry of active citizens, families, places of worship, dedicated professions and independent associations. Government must become the servant of society. Only then will we be able to realise the mission that Iain Duncan Smith has given the Conservative party: the renewal of society.

1   In an interview with *Woman's Own*, 31 October 1987

2   David Page, *Communities in the balance: The reality of social exclusion on housing estates*, Joseph Rowntree Foundation, November 2000

3   National Federation of Community Organisations, *The Visible Difference*, May 2002

4   18 May 2002, Perth

The new contours of
British politics

David Willetts

David Willetts is Shadow Work and Pensions Secretary and MP for Havant. He has worked at HM Treasury, the Downing Street Policy Unit, and as Director of Studies at the Centre for Policy Studies. He has written widely on economic and social policy. He is a Visiting Fellow at Nuffield College, Oxford, and a member of the Board of the British Council. He is married with two school-age children.

Lessons from the One Nation Hearings

However much we think we know from debating policy in Parliament or by tackling the problems faced by our own constituents, there is still much more to learn by gaining first-hand experience of the sheer diversity of social challenges across Britain. That is what Conservative MPs have been trying to do through the series of One Nation Hearings that I initiated in

February. These Hearings have so far taken me to nearly twenty varied projects including an Alcoholics Anonymous meeting in Birmingham; a hostel for recovering drug addicts in Kent; and a 24-hour crisis centre for people with mental health problems in north London. Each one of these One Nation Hearings has taught me the most basic lesson of all: that however much you think you know there is always more to learn. Some other specific observations stand out.

Firstly, I have a renewed respect for the many unsung heroes working for little or no pay throughout Britain. Sometimes they might be donating a few hours a week to a local charity. Others might be fully committed social entrepreneurs investing an enormous amount of energy into running innovative projects for drug abusers, homeless people or at-risk teenagers. Many, because of the sheer magnitude of their personal commitment, are able to help turn around the lives of a drug abuser or an alcoholic in a way that would be very difficult for a conventional professional. All of them appreciate the public services and their essential role in sustaining people through some very bad times. But when it comes, for example, to getting alcoholics to confront the reality of what is happening in their lives and to change them for the better there is no help more powerful than someone motivated by a compelling personal mission. And often this mission comes from either having triumphed over such an experience themselves or through a personal religious conviction to love a neighbour in need.

Secondly, in Kent I saw one of the most imaginative anti-dependency programmes of any local authority in Britain. One of the most stark and crude measures of dependency is how much is being spent on benefits. If a local authority can effectively tackle social problems we should see a reduction of dependence on means-tested welfare benefits. This is the philosophy behind an imaginative addition to the normal public service agreement between local and central government that has been pioneered by Kent County Council's Conservative leadership. If Kent County Council can show that its unique set of social independence projects have reduced expenditure on welfare below what it might otherwise have been, then some of the savings will be returned by the Treasury to Kent County Council. The real reward, of course, is the mending of broken lives but the strategy also offers the whole of Kent the possibility of investing in higher quality local services and securing greater economic vitality across the county.

Thirdly, many of the volunteers and charities that I have been meeting have criticised the sheer complexity of the grant application process they have to navigate. I am sure that every specific new initiative launched by ministers comes with the best of intentions. But many of them allocate funds by an elaborate system of competitive bidding that absorbs a massive amount of the time and energy of some of the most active citizens in Britain's hard-pressed communities. Every hour a community worker spends navigating the complex grant application process is another hour that cannot be given to the people who need help most.

These are just three snapshots from the early One Nation Hearings: (1) highly motivated active citizens leading the way in repairing broken lives; (2) an innovative scheme for rewarding a local authority if it can help hard-to-employ people achieve independence; and (3) the complex and onerous burden on community-based charities bidding for packets of public money. A strong theme emerges that links these particular findings. And that theme is the incredible clumsiness of the state, however well intentioned, when it comes to tackling the sheer intricacy of social problems. The state can seem so thick-fingered and ignorant to the poverty-fighters on the frontline. It's like a man trying to repair a cobweb with his own bare hands. By far the most effective schemes are local, discretionary and flexible. They are not uniform, national or rule-bound. This is an important lesson we must apply as we look afresh at our social policies.

In the past the Conservative response to such evidence appeared to be that there was nothing that the state could do in these circumstances. It was all a matter of the individual sorting his life out, perhaps assisted by an occasional local charity. But we cannot wash our hands of our fellow citizens who find themselves in the most desperate of circumstances. We can't tell them to pull their socks up while we walk away. We have a responsibility to our fellow citizens and it includes a responsibility that can only be discharged through effective public policy as well as through personal and private action. The focus of that effective public policy action will, however, be support for the local and people-sized institutions that serve Britain's hardest-pressed communities.

The lessons of economic reform in the former Soviet Union

Travelling back ten years and nearly 2,000 miles to Moscow in the early 1990s we find communism collapsed and a wholesale rejection of the centrally planned economy. Free-market economists arrived in the old Soviet Union determined to convert it into a successful market economy. They achieved modest successes but the experience of free-market reformers in the former Soviet Union has generally not been a happy one. They found it far more difficult to create the institutions of a market economy than they expected. Thus, optimism was understandable. After all there is a universal instinct to truck, barter and exchange. We can trade internationally with countries with very different cultures from our own. But when it comes to creating a properly functioning market economy there are limits to what economic policy can do on its own. After more than eighty years of communism the culture and the institutions necessary to sustain a market economy had gone. Just as the communists had destroyed the physical environment of old Russia they had also exhausted its moral capital. The result was a Wild West-style economy distorted by mafia bullies, capricious courts, corrupt politicians and aggressive financial industrial groups. The collapse of the Soviet Union – which at first was taken as a victory for the market economy – ended up teaching us a rather more complicated lesson. Of course we need a modern market economy but it can only survive if it is underpinned by non-market values that define the limits to competition and market transactions. There are some things you can't sell and shouldn't be allowed to. Any market economy, in order to survive, needs to operate within a social framework that supports and sustains it.

It might seem a long way from Iain Duncan Smith's One Nation Hearings to the failure of economic reform in the old Soviet Union. But there is a rather important connection and it is what we now call civil society or, even more fashionably, social capital. Civil society consists of all the institutions and patterns of behaviour that are bigger than any one individual but are not part of the public sector. In fact they are just about everything that gives life its meaning. We are not individual atoms floating around in a vacuum. Nor are we creatures to be moulded by politicians in accordance with their whims. We are not, despite Labour's fantasies, a region-alist country. But we are certainly localist with strong ties of attachment to our town or our county. We all know our local hospital even if we do not know the name of the latest Government creation that is supposed to finance it. We all know the local school even if we are not sure about the local education authority. And most of us will feel an obligation to our neighbours even if we think too much of our taxes is spent on the welfare state. The challenge for modern Conservatives is to harness these deep-seated and powerful human instincts to a policy agenda for government.

The new contours of political debate

What we are looking at here are the contours of the intellectual battleground over which the political parties are going to fight for years to come. Let me try to put this in a grossly simplified way. Traditionally Labour was the party of big government. We have come to be seen as the party that believes that there is no such thing as society; only the individual pursuing his or her economic self-interest. But what really matters most of all to Conservatives is everything in between the individual and the state. It's how we sustain and support that rich social architecture that is the real challenge for politics today.

Some people in the Labour Party have spotted this. Frank Field has great moral authority because he grasped the issue earlier than most. And in the past Tony Blair talked about community and partnership with the voluntary sector in a way that suggested that he too had understood the point. But the reality of Labour in office has been very different from what was promised.

The tragedy has been that in using the very language of partnership with the voluntary sector this Labour Government has, despite its best intentions, been weakening it still further. The bid culture is a real threat to any capacity for local discretion and local judgement. And in their clumsy agenda for health and education they have shown they have less understanding of what it means to be a professional than perhaps any previous Government in history. They are so nervous and uncertain about the family that we have had complete paralysis when it comes to, for instance, reforming family law. Whilst the more thoughtful advisers around Tony Blair produce reports on social capital the reality is that they have been destroying it. In many ways New Labour is a more materialist party than Conservatives were ever accused of being in the 1980s. Labour's materialist bias is evident in their one-dimensional approach to child poverty.

The real problem with Tony Blair's child poverty target is that it is exclusively financial. Eliminating poverty is defined by ministers as no children in families with less than 60% of median income. They appear to believe they will eliminate poverty with extra spending on welfare benefits. Of course, money is important. But all the evidence from all the post-war attempts at eliminating poverty is that it can't be done by expanding benefits. What if a family that does receive extra money is unable to let their children out to play because there are drug users' syringes on the stairwell outside their flat? And what if their children are unable to learn because of an endlessly changing cast of supply teachers at the local school? And what if they come from a broken home without stability and love? Conservatives understand that that is poverty, too. Conservatives can and must show that we can do better in fighting the reality of poverty and the reality of community breakdown.

I have long believed that the future for our party is as the party which stands for not just the individual on his or her own, but the individual in voluntary association with others. Individuals need not just work together through the state or through a commercial enterprise. They can also do so through all the rich variety of civic institutions which have historically been one of the most distinctive features of our country. I called this civic conservatism. Oliver Letwin gave it the rather better name of the neighbourly society. That must be the way ahead for our party. It is the way ahead for our most hard-pressed neighbourhoods.

The new wave of compassionate conservatism

Rick Santorum

Senator Rick Santorum from Pennsylvania has served in the United States Senate since January 1995. Now the third-ranking Republican in the Senate, as Conference Chairman, Senator Santorum directs the communications operations of Senate Republicans. He is best known for his commitment to family values, faith-based initiatives and wealth creation for the poor. He is a staunch defender of the culture of life and has pioneered the fight against partial-birth abortion and cloning. Senator Santorum and his wife, Karen, are the parents of seven children.

President Bush has made compassionate conservatism the foundation of his political platform. He believes his administration has a responsibility to help people to help other people. Therefore, this help comes not from increasing the government's power and influence on people's lives. Rather, the President's preferred solution is to look first to faith-based organisations, charities and community groups that have shown their ability to save and change lives.

Community-based and pro-family initiatives

Since his election, President Bush has made compassionate conservatism a priority. For that, I am thankful. I share the heart of his compassionate conservatism – his commitment to faith-based initiatives, and rhetorical focus on charities and community groups that have shown their ability to save and change lives. The President has also rightly emphasised the importance of teaching character in our schools and the promotion of responsible father-hood. Establishing a cultural acceptance of the importance of fathers is essential. The leading feminist Gloria Steinem once infamously remarked that 'a woman needs a man like a fish needs a bicycle'. When Ms Steinem got married over a year ago we can be forgiven for suggesting that the fish got its bicycle. George W Bush has not had to undertake any change of heart on family policy and recently said: 'Strong marriages and stable families are incredibly good for children, and stable families should be the central goal of American welfare policy.'[1]

In the 1980s Ronald Reagan and Margaret Thatcher pursued parallel economic revolutions. In the twenty-first century the British Conservative and American Republican parties are sharing a new agenda. This new agenda has deep roots within the one-nation tradition founded by Benjamin Disraeli and has been powerfully updated with the twelve principles in this book.

The compassionate conservative agenda affirms the importance of voluntarism, character and virtue: all dimensions that are essential to a good and sustainable society and dimensions that have been neglected by the political Left.

This first phase of the President's compassionate conservatism has been very successful. However, 'compassionate conservatism' is best defined through efforts to address the needs of the poor, rather than by simply linking it to any issue that shows we 'care'. We must start to narrow the gap between the rich and the poor so that more low-income Americans can begin to share in the American dream. That is why we need to begin a second phase that focuses on transforming poverty in America.

Historically, my involvement in fashioning this agenda began in 1993–4 when I began working on welfare. In 1995, Congressmen Dan Coats, Jim Talent, J C Watts and I felt it was critical to create a venue for conservatives who wanted to promote civil society, especially faith and community-based initiatives. The purpose of this was to counter the Left's claim that they alone care for the poor. We created the Renewal Alliance and introduced the REAL LIFE initiative (Renewal, Empowerment, Education for Life) to create a focused legislative programme based on conservative principles that addressed the needs of low-income families and communities.[2]

Reducing barriers to wealth creation for the poor

One of the primary causes of poverty that is overlooked is access to capital and barriers to wealth creation. Increased income is one way for families and communities to climb out of poverty. Wealth creation is another. Wealth allows for ownership, fosters self-reliance and independence, and creates jobs. Wealth in turn creates more wealth. Initiatives that encourage individual wealth creation are imperative to closing the gap between the rich and the poor. Among these initiatives are increasing savings, social security assets, home ownership and access to capital.

Savings

Providing low-income families with incentives to save is one way to shrink the growing gap between the rich and the poor. Non-profit groups throughout the United States have launched innovative private programmes that are successfully helping people who have never had a bank account. Through Individual Development Accounts (IDAs)[3], banks and credit unions offer special savings accounts to low-income Americans and match their deposits dollar for dollar. In return, participants take an economic literacy course and commit to using their savings to buy a home, upgrade their education or start a business. Also, through an IDA provision in the Savings Opportunity and Charitable Giving Act, IDA access will be expanded across the country, giving a tax credit to financial institutions that will help the impoverished.

Personal retirement accounts

Another means of creating personal wealth for low-income Americans is through fiscally sustainable and actuarially sound

Social Security reform. Social Security's financing challenges are well known and have been studied extensively. The President's Commission to Strengthen Social Security (CSSS)[4] was instrumental in further analysing the current programme's fiscal shortfalls and benefit inequalities. Many people never become eligible for Social Security benefits because they do not have enough years of contributions to earn their own benefits. Moreover, lower-income individuals tend to have shorter life expectancies and spend a greater portion of their lives contributing to Social Security and a smaller portion collecting from it. The options of raising taxes or drastically reducing promised benefits proportionately affect the poor and low-income workers who contribute to the system.

However, for the first time in the programme's history, there is a path towards reform that would better protect low-income individuals and families and offer them the opportunity to accumulate wealth: the creation of voluntary personal retirement accounts (PRAs). PRAs can serve as a mechanism to pre-fund a portion of future Social Security benefits. PRAs would provide low-income workers with retirement income buttressed by a strong safety net benefit that would sustain them better than the current system. And for the first time, it would allow them to bequeath a portion of their 'contributions' (personal savings) to their children.

Home ownership
Home ownership is another pivotal avenue for wealth creation. For many low-income Americans, home ownership is the signal

that they have made it into the economic mainstream. But unfortunately for too many, the dream of owning one's home seems hopelessly out of reach. It is important that we look for ways to improve the asset base of low-income Americans so they can buy their own home.

As previously discussed, IDAs can be expanded to help more American families save for the down payment on a home. Currently, there is a bipartisan consensus in support of home ownership, whether it is through down-payment assistance programmes sponsored by local governments or the federal income tax deduction for mortgage interest. Congress has chartered two government-sponsored enterprises known as 'Fannie Mae' and 'Freddie Mac'. These enterprises make home ownership possible for more Americans by creating an efficient secondary mortgage market to increase the funding available to lenders. The Federal Housing Administration (FHA) has also helped more families purchase homes by lowering the amount required for down payment. Home Investment Partnership (HOME) programmes are also key components to neighbour-hood revitalisation. HOME makes grants available to local governments that provide affordable housing for low-income renters and owners through new construction, rehabilitation, and property acquisition.

Access to entrepreneurial capital
Furthermore, access to capital is a critical way of creating wealth. Robert Friedman and Ray Boshara have written of the impor-

tance of America's working-poor families being enabled to 'build assets, not just income; empower them to own, not just owe; view them as savers, producers, and entrepreneurs, not just recipients, borrowers, and trainees. In other words, through opportunities to save and acquire assets, invite low-income working Americans to be participants in the American economy, rather than recipients of its excesses.'[5] This can be achieved through the American Community Renewal and New Markets Empowerment Act that I introduced. This comprehensive bill, which includes IDAs, creates economic incentives for investment in low-income communities and enhances educational, home-ownership, and affordable housing opportunities in these areas. Also, the Community Development Block Grant (CDBG) programme provides flexible federal funding to local recipients, who select the most appropriate programmes to fight poverty and spur economic growth among the poor.

Empowering vulnerable people

Through these innovative methods of wealth creation the Republican Party will redefine compassion, countering the Left's false claim that they are the only party who truly cares for the poor. Conservatives will be branding compassionate conservatism as something unique and genuine that will be pivotal for outreach for African-Americans, Hispanics and other immigrants. Compassionate conservatism is definitely the future of the Republican Party and, I hope, Britain's Conservative Party, too. I strongly agree with Iain Duncan

Smith's statement that 'a nation that leaves its vulnerable behind, diminishes its own future'.[6] The Conservative leader's mission to empower vulnerable people will also, I believe, have great electoral potency.

The new proposals for wealth creation will help fulfill the President's desire to 'rally the armies of compassion in our communities to fight a very different war against poverty and hopelessness, a daily battle waged house to house and heart by heart'. The American Dream will finally be within the reach of many low-income Americans. As President Bush stated in his 'Duty of Hope' speech delivered in Indianapolis on 22 July 1999:

> This will not be the failed compassion of towering, distant bureaucracies. On the contrary, it will be a government that serves those who are serving their neighbours . . . It will be a government that both knows its limits, and shows its heart. And it will be a government truly by the people and for the people.

1   George W Bush, Radio address to the nation, 11 May 2002

2   www.senate.gov/~santorum/real/real.html

3   www.idanetwork.org

4   www.csss.gov

5   Robert Freidman and Roy Boshara, The Corporation for Enterprise Development, www.cfed.gov

6   Iain Duncan Smith, speech to the Conservative Party Spring Forum, Harrogate, 24 March 2002

Politics on a human scale

John Hayes

John Hayes has been Member of Parliament for South Holland and the Deepings since 1997. A former Nottinghamshire County Councillor and Vice Chairman of the Conservative Party, he is now Shadow Minister for Agriculture. John is co-chairman of the All-Party Disability Committee. He is married with one son.

Redefining our mission
For too long politicians have assumed that good economics equals good politics; they have behaved as though standard of living and quality of life are synonymous.

The view that endless material advance is the utopia to which all policy should be directed has dominated political debate for fifty or so years. This is a reductionist view of politics that ignores all those components necessary to a balanced quality of life that do not relate to economic well-being.

Because quality of life has awkward associations with values and morals it became convenient for politicians to retreat to the safer ground of managing the public purse and advocacy of ever greater material consumption.

The flight by most politicians from all those areas of legitimate political and cultural concern – 'social continuity, national identity and tradition upon which durable political order depends'[1] and which underpin a civilised way of life – has left little opportunity to debate the idea of community or the salience of localness. In the political mainstream there has been scant consideration of the problem of scale and too little debate about the political and economic alternatives to selfish materialism fed by ever larger economic and political structures.

British Conservatives recognise that man is a social creature and that only a certain kind of responsible individualism is compatible with a free society.

President George W Bush has identified a parallel challenge for his nation. In his post-September 11th State of the Union Address he observed:

> We were reminded that we are citizens, with obligations to each other, to our country, and to history. We began to think less of the goods we can accumulate, and more about the good we can do... We have glimpsed what a new culture of responsibility could look like. We want to be a nation that serves goals larger than self.[2]

It is in localism and community that the counter-arguments to selfish materialism are located. It is in people-sized institutions like the family, church and school that, from childhood onwards, we learn civility and courtesy, how to give and to share, so our 'other-regarding instincts' are fostered in order to overcome our 'natural self-regarding instincts'.[3]

The anxieties of our age

The Conservative Party will deserve the British people's trust when it can again show that it understands the real hopes and fears of people throughout Britain.

International insecurity is the stuff of nightmares, but there are profound domestic anxieties that can no longer be ignored.

First, we know that the material success that most of us enjoy is not the same as true fulfilment. Yes, it is welcome but the hours committed to generating income are increasingly onerous, leaving us with little time for family, friends and culture. Even the promise of pursuing 'greater things' during retirement is clouded by increasing uncertainty about pensions. Meanwhile the enjoyment of daily life is routinely diminished by everyday incivility and increasingly by the fear and reality of violent crime.

Second, economic opportunity and security have yet to reach many millions of Britons. Whilst few, even the prosperous, are unfamiliar with the social ills associated with drug use, family breakdown and crime, these problems are cruelly concentrated in the poorest areas where they underpin an inter-generational absence of economic opportunity. In the short term, society can immorally choose to ignore or manage social decay. Given its

70

spread, there will soon be no option but to address it.

The third anxiety centres on decreasing confidence in the willingness, or even ability, of those who wield power, and the processes which they drive, to maintain the foundations upon which quality of life is built. Joseph Schumpeter has highlighted the 'contradictions' of capitalism and its tendency, for example, to undermine those very patterns of behaviour (such as trust, thrift and delayed gratification) that also determine its vitality.

For Conservatives something beyond capitalism must invest in and nourish the social capital upon which a successful marriage between civil society and free enterprise depends.

A new purpose for capitalism and democracy

Capitalism as an economic system cannot be detached from the cultural context in which it operates. The most important challenges we face are not economic, they are social and cultural; those which Peter Hitchens describes as 'the decay of obligation, duty and morality'.[4] Professor Michael Novak calls us to recognise that 'prior to economics is politics and prior to politics is culture'.[5] Our response to today's anxieties must not be to shackle democracy or capitalism but to direct them to new purposes. For though big business and government often represent powerful vested interests, change is possible in a free society of free people:

> What is distinctive about the human spirit is its capacity
> for seeing through its decadence... The human being
> can invent a new horizon for his or her future, individual

71

by individual, and in sufficient numbers to generate cultural renewal.'[6]

But this great task of providing a new purpose for capitalism and democracy cannot be pursued at a pan-national level. It has to be conceived in the organisations and communities that are shaped and best understood by free people. The institutions and communities that operate in the knowledge that the anxieties and hopes of every person matter. These institutions tend to be small and accessible.

Conservatives must now be bold enough to lead a debate about scale, community and the localisation of power. The interests of trans-national capital, particularly its need for limitless flexibility and mobility, may sometimes 'mitigate against the sense of community in neighbourhoods and the solidarity of the extended family'.[7] We need to develop policies in response to these pressures.

Scale, localism and diversity

Our task will not be easy. Our opponents are not just in Government – they are the new Establishment. An Establishment embedded in the media, universities and the welfare system which has a vested interest in the self-perpetuation of remote bureaucracies.

Those who view politics as 'discovering final and complete solutions to all human problems'[8] seek big ideas and big structures to deliver them. Impatient with the imperfections of humankind and its endeavours, they are seduced by the tidiness and wholeness of pan-national or trans-national grand designs. Such theorists claim that only by countering man's haphazard efforts at self-government with a centralised and standardised model can their brave new world be built.

Conservatives have a more humble view of the efficacy of government. We see 'politics as an activity concerned with the management and mitigation of tensions inherent in human existence'.[9] So we appreciate that 'men and therefore the structures by which they govern themselves are organisms not mechanisms and should not be made to fit a grand design'.[10]

Big government's advocates also suggest it guarantees equity and comparability. But the glory of trusting local people to run their own affairs is that the solutions they devise will be sensitive to local needs and different from one village, town, city or nation to another. The diversity that emerges from giving communities the power and resources to innovate is of much greater value than the knowledge that your neighbourhood will be assessed in the same way as every other neighbourhood. It is of debatable value to the people of Penzance to measure the public services they receive against those of the citizens of Peterborough, still less Pisa! International and national comparisons of local services are certainly not a justification for the suffocation of local autonomy that has been a feature of public policy for the last fifty years.

Centralisation is not inevitable

Perhaps the greatest success of our opponents has been to convince many that the centralising trend, by which local communities retain little influence over their own affairs, and by which nations surrender power to supra-national institutions, is inevitable and unstoppable. This determinist view of humanity is fundamentally flawed. It assumes that man is merely acting out a script over which he has no influence. In fact there is no predetermined course of history. The only limits on our ability to shape our destinies spring from God-given human nature.

But big government is not the only threat to our way of life. Many soulless and rootless big businesses demonstrate little loyalty to local producers and only the minimum necessary commitment to consumers. The ubiquity fostered by multinationals is an aesthetic disaster. Its consequence has been the standardisation of our townscapes – everywhere the same shop fronts selling the same products. Local delicacies are replaced by the predictable uniform flavour of a bland burger supplied by the same corporation operating from Bournemouth to Borneo.

The link between political and business elites is founded – in addition to a shared preoccupation with mediocre uniformity – on an assumption that the supreme challenge for man is the drive towards ever greater economic growth and the relentless pursuit of material self-interest. To the trans-national corporation this assumption is a necessary prerequisite to their profit-driven expansion. To the political pan-nationalists universal prosperity is seen as the most likely guarantee of world peace. One of the most commonly vaunted and facile arguments for transferring more power to the EU is that this will ensure no repetition of European conflagration. The notion that economic prosperity is the guarantee of peace is convincingly refuted by Schumacher, who argues that 'it is chimerical to build on economic foundations which, in turn, rest on the systematic cultivation of greed and envy, the very forces which drive men into conflict'.[11] Even a cursory study of world history illustrates that central domination and the attempt to extinguish local traditions is a frequent cause of conflict.

Localism and creativity are natural allies

Big government, big business and big media are all suffocating – in different ways and with different motives – local diversity.

Yet New Labour has exacerbated the problems of scale and uniformity because it misunderstands and undervalues diversity and localism. Mr Blair has presided over a massive increase in red tape and a significant increase in the complexity of the regulatory burden. By design or accident this, like workplace-administered tax credits, has hugely favoured big over small business. Big business – although it may not always like government regulation – absorbs it more easily.

The BBC is another example of a big corporation that, whilst often providing high-quality services, suffocates diversity. There have been many complaints that its recent expansion of digital services, in particular, has threatened independent arts and ethnic broadcasters. The BBC is dominated by a liberal worldview that means that its monopoly position in key areas is undemocratic and a cause for real concern. A Government committed to diversity and localism would not allow the BBC to pursue such anti-competitive behaviour.

Big government is, of course, also a major offender in its own right. The welfare state too often delivers crude 'one-size-fits-all' solutions, effectively prohibiting communities from delivering alternative welfare models more sensitive to local needs. The focus of dutiful professionals in the great public services, typically against their own instincts and judgement, is directed away from their patients and pupils and towards meeting government's national plans and targets. Only that which can be reduced to a set of statistics appears to be valued. Government funds only those parts of the voluntary sector that share its ethos. Any drugs charity must therefore be supportive of the Government's lax attitude to cannabis or sacrifice its funding. Any relationship education charity that chooses to emphasise marriage is defunded. Pregnancy crisis services that want to help women keep their babies rather than encourage abortion are ignored by those holding the purse strings.

This debate represents not only a conflict between big and small, but also a clash between ubiquity and diversity, between standardisation and creativity.

Politics on a human scale

During the eighteen years of Conservative government we were frequently caricatured by our opponents as favouring big business, encouraging greed and ignoring those in most need. That this is not a fair analysis of that period is less important than the fact that it has become the received wisdom. This popular misconception of our record in office is the electoral context in which we now operate.

Our re-engagement in debates about cultural change, scale, community and sustainability is vital. It is vital not just because these matters are central to a holistic Conservative perspective, but also because, through the renewal of a distinctively Conservative philosophy, we will be recast and our credibility restored in the eyes of the electorate. Our focus on these issues will match the preoccupations of a people who see their standard of living as only one part of a decent quality of life.

Conservatives should reject the social liberalism of New Labour that weakens the family and the other institutions that best protect children from drugs, delinquency and despair.

Conservatives should also realise that for an electorate beset by uncertainties and insecurities will not be reassured by a dated neo-liberal reaction that has little to offer beyond unbridled individualism.

The aim of Conservative policy should, therefore, be the reinvigoration of society – its institutions and its values. By so doing the sense of local and national identity so long undermined by our opponents will be renewed.

Conservatives must advance beyond the confining concentration on material self-interest. Conservatives must champion a new politics that serves society and respects communities by releasing their power to innovate.

We must once again be the champions of politics on a human scale.

---

1   Roger Scruton, *Conservative Thoughts*, The Claridge Press 1988

2   George W Bush, The State of the Union Address, 2002

3   Michael Novak, Capitalism and the Human Spirit, The Public Interest, Spring 2002

4   Peter Hitchens, *The Abolition of Britain*, Quartet Books 1999

5   Michael Novak, op. cit.

6   Ibid.

7   Robin Harris, *The Conservative Community – The roots of Thatcherism and its future*, Centre for Policy Studies 1989

8   David J Levy, The Politics of Welfare, Salisbury Review, October 1985

9   Ibid.

10 Robert Cranbourne, *Allegiance: The Nation State, Parliament and Prosperity*, Politeia 1999

11 E F Schumacher, *Small is Beautiful*, Blond and Briggs, 1975

Part three

Twelve principles of compassionate conservatism

The twelve principles of compassionate conservatism

At the start of each chapter in this third part of the book David McLetchie MSP provides brief introductions to each of the twelve principles. Individual authors then apply that principle to one area of public policy.

David McLetchie is the Leader of the Conservative Group in the Scottish Parliament and one of the regional list MSPs for Lothian. Prior to entering Parliament in 1999 he was a solicitor in private practice and worked with a number of charities and voluntary groups. He is married to Sheila, a theatre nurse at Edinburgh Royal Infirmary.

One

Every person has dignity and potential

Compassionate Conservatives will promote one nation in which people of every walk of life are welcomed into the full life of society. Because all human life is of infinite value, a good society will help people fulfil their potential and aspirations. For this reason one nation Conservatives cannot be indifferent to self-destructive forms of behaviour.

Overleaf Ian McGill and Colin Robertson apply this principle to drug addiction.

Drugs undermine
human dignity

Iain McGill and Colin Robertson

Iain McGill began his career as a postman, before getting involved in a variety of humanitarian projects including six months in a children's hospice in Albania and flood rescue work in Mozambique. He now works with homeless people in Edinburgh, bringing him into daily contact with addiction problems of all kinds.

Colin Robertson works for the Scottish Conservative and Unionist Party in the Press and Research Unit, specialising in education issues. In his spare time Colin runs the Company Section at his local Boys' Brigade and is involved in other youth work projects. He is married and lives in Leith, Edinburgh.

The idea of human dignity, the innate and infinite worth of every individual is a powerful idea common to many religious and political traditions. It has inspired some of the great campaigns for justice and freedom, from the struggle against slavery in the nineteenth century to the fight against eugenics in the twentieth. But while human dignity is a standard to which we rally in response to naked bigotry, all too often it is forgotten when more insidious threats arise. One such threat is that of drug abuse. There is a lot of talk about the differences between 'soft' drugs and 'hard' drugs, but one thing they all have in common is that, in all sorts of ways, they rob their users of dignity. Any one who thinks that this is a rather precious point to make should survey the ruins of a drug policy that pays little heed to human dignity – Britain's drug policy.

Everyone is vulnerable to drugs

It is easy to stereotype and pigeonhole drug addicts but the truth is everybody is vulnerable. There is no entry exam to sit, no age limit, no sexual or racial discrimination. All of us are potential victims. When we are talking about victims we don't just mean the addicts themselves, but their family and friends, who are all affected by an individual's problems with addiction, as are neighbours and work colleagues. Of course, there are some people who are more vulnerable than others – people in prisons, young offenders, the homeless, children raised by addicts, those who suffer stress in work or study, those who have suffered from abusive relationships, those who suffer from chronic pain or emotional anguish. We all know people in these situations, which is why drug addiction has the potential to affect us all. It is often only once somebody beats their addiction that they see the pain they have caused their loved ones, because when someone is trapped in their addiction the drug becomes the most important thing to them; everything else becomes secondary. Thus drugs not only rob the user of dignity, but also stop the user from recognising the dignity of others.

Writing people off

Drug policy in this country is informed by the 'harm reduction' philosophy, which, rather than focusing on the drug abuse itself, is more concerned with reducing the harmful side-effects – in particular crime and health problems. The flaw in this approach is that even if it succeeds on its own terms – a big if – it does not address the addict's loss of dignity, which is a fact of the addiction. And in a further assault on the ideal of human dignity, the advocates of harm reduction assume that drug abuse is inevitable, even natural, especially amongst certain groups.

For instance, this is the advice to young people from a Home Office-funded website aimed at teenagers: 'If you're going to do drugs then first be aware of the risks involved. Knowing the facts may not protect you from a bad time, but it's better to be clued up than clueless.'[1] It all seems so reasonable, but what's the first message that young people take away from this and countless other drug education resources? What does it do to teenagers to be told by authority figures that not only are they likely to do drugs, but that nothing better is expected from them?

By writing people off like this, the danger is that outside efforts go into containing the problem, not helping individuals to be all that they can be. This is an attitude taken to students who are vulnerable as they move to a new place and have new pressures and freedoms placed upon them like the pressure of exams, making ends meet, to conform, to fit in and find new friends. These can all take their toll and some find a release, for a time, in drugs. Better education in our colleges and universities on the very real risks involved in getting mixed up in the drugs scene, as well as training for tutors on the warning signs, could make a difference. But it won't happen if drug abuse by students is just seen as a rite of passage. Even less is expected of Britain's prison population. Drugs are freely available in many institutions, and a lot of people develop habits while in jail. The drugs provide an escape from the depressing, monotonous existence experienced by many inmates. A spell inside should be a great opportunity for a prisoner to get off drugs but this is not happening. The failure of the authorities to prevent drugs being available inside the penal system is almost inevitable once an attitude of writing people off has taken hold.

Lambeth, New York, Amsterdam

Sometimes an entire community can be written off. This is true of Lambeth where the 'softly, softly' policy of the police is not to prosecute people for possession of cannabis. It has been described as an 'experiment', but surely to be meaningful we should have a zero-tolerance policy in another area and a comparison of the results. Nevertheless, the results of the 'softly, softly' approach are already becoming clear in Lambeth. Speaking in the House of Commons, local MP Kate Hoey pointed out that since the experiment began there were:

more drug dealers on the street than ever, many young
children are going to school in the morning zonked out
on a very hard kind of cannabis and more and more
residents are being harassed and almost attacked by drug
dealers on their way home from work.

In conclusion she asked whether:

the Prime Minister will do something about cleaning up
these gangs of criminals and stick up for decent law-
abiding citizens and residents who are fed up being
experimented on.[2]

One place that has tried the opposite approach is New York City,
where the former mayor Rudolph Giuliani implemented his
'broken windows' policy, which succeeded in slashing crime rates
by targeting minor anti-social offences. When he visited Britain
to receive an honorary knighthood he criticised the relaxed
attitude to cannabis in Lambeth:

Marijuana caused a lot of the violence we had. I would
encourage the police to arrest as many of them [drug
users] as possible.

On cannabis use he said:

It is not a victimless crime, it leads to other bigger, more

violent crimes. Anyone should be arrested for the use of
marijuana.[3]

Whole essays could be written comparing drug law enforcement
in London and New York. But ultimately it is the latter that
affirms human dignity because it expects the best from people.
Perhaps the instigators of the Lambeth experiment should state
just what their expectations are of the communities they have
singled out for experimentation.

However, Lambeth will not be on its own for long. The
Government has decided to downgrade cannabis from a Class B
drug to a Class C drug, effectively extending the Lambeth experiment nationwide. The Government claims that this will help the
police win the war against hard drugs. But the signs from Lambeth
are not encouraging, nor is the example of Holland, where cannabis
use is decriminalised but which is a European centre for the abuse,
manufacture and trafficking of hard drugs. Dutch drugs policy also
provides an example of what goes wrong when the principle of
human dignity is left out of the equation. These are the revealing
words of Dr Ernst Buning of the Dutch Ministry of Health, a key
figure in the country's drugs policy establishment:

> There are young people who abuse soft drugs. Particularly
> those that have this high THC [the psychoactive ingre-
> dient in cannabis]. The place that cannabis takes in their
> lives becomes so dominant they don't have space for the
> other important things in life. They crawl out of bed in

the morning, grab a joint, don't work, smoke another joint. They don't know what to do with their lives. I don't want to call it a drug problem because if I do, then we have to get into a discussion that cannabis is dangerous, that sometimes you can't use it without doing damage to your health or your psyche. The moment we say, 'there are people who have problems with soft drugs' our critics will jump on us, so it makes it a little bit difficult for us to be objective on this matter.[4]

The harm reduction approach is essentially a policy of denial, of pretending that the wasted potential of so many people doesn't matter so long as the doctors contain the medical effects and the police contain the criminal effects. But being in denial about the root causes undermines even the limited ambitions of the policy of harm reduction, as the Amsterdam Police Commissioner, Jelle Kuiper, warns:

As long as our political class tries to pretend that soft drugs do not create dependence, we are going to go on being confronted daily with problems that officially do not exist. We are aware of an enormous number of young people strongly dependent on soft drugs, with all the consequences that has.[5]

Methadone nation
The same disregard for human dignity applies to the care of

hard-drug addicts in Holland. While the Dutch emphasis is on 'treatment', other countries like Sweden stress rehabilitation.[6] In other words, the overriding objective in Holland is to stop drug addicts coming to harm (or at least to minimise harm), while in Sweden it is to stop drug addicts using drugs. The rising average age of Holland's junkies is frequently cited by the pro-liberalisers in support of the harm reduction approach.[7] They imply that this down to its success in reducing drug-related deaths and/or keeping younger people off hard drugs. But in the absence of evidence for either the former or the latter, a third explanation presents itself: that the Dutch system has become so adept at patching up its drug addicts that addiction can be maintained into middle age. It takes a desperately poor regard for human dignity to look upon this 'achievement' as progress.

The mother's milk of the Dutch treatment system is the heroin substitute, methadone. Britain too relies heavily on a methadone programme which has failed and is routinely abused by addicts. Despite the fact that it is supposed to be a controlled substance, methadone is traded in the streets and people regularly die of overdoses.[8] By continuing down this path, the NHS is making the problem worse, not better. It increases the amount of hard drugs on the street. It creates new dependencies for people instead of helping them to break free from the addiction of opiate-based drugs. Methadone addiction is a harder habit to break than heroin.

The regulation of the programme must be tightened up. It is far too easy to get a prescription and there is far too little supervision of what is happening to the drug when the addict collects it from the pharmacist. But even for legitimate users, the methadone programme is flawed and is in need of a radical overhaul. While methadone can be a valuable tool in the stabilisation, detoxification and rehabilitation of people with addictions, the current regime keeps people trapped in their addictions. There is much to learn from Sweden where a whole range of safeguards ensures that the system is not abused. It is much tougher to get a prescription for a start, and much easier to have it taken from you if you do abuse the system.[9] Admission depends on a documented history of compulsive intravenous abuse of opiates of at least four years. Clients that engage in violent behaviour, deal drugs, get convicted of a crime or misuse their prescription are expelled. The same goes for clients who use drugs or drink on top of their methadone, which is the tolerated and self-defeating norm in Britain.

In Sweden, methadone treatment is a last resort and thus provision for detox and rehab is made accordingly. A lot of our problems in the UK stem from a lack of such facilities. The ones we have are struggling with outdated methods of funding from social services departments and waiting lists of between eight and twelve weeks for a place. These delays are unacceptable; especially as methadone is prescribed as a bridging measure so that when places do become available they are often rejected in favour of continuing methadone dependency. There is something seriously wrong with a system that makes it easy to surrender to drugs but frustrates the best intentions of vulnerable people. As soon as an addict decides that they want to get clean they should be afforded all the help society can possibly offer. That means a place in a rehab/detox unit at the moment of need rather than weeks or months later. It is truly shocking that funding delays should be allowed to come between a human being and what it takes to save them from addiction, prison or even death.

Judge the results, not the method

Improving access to detox and rehab would be an enormous stride forward, but we must also improve the range of options available. Every drug addict is an individual. There is no one-size-fits-all system of assistance. What works for some may not work for others. A truly tolerant society should value a diversity of solutions. If the state wishes to help the vulnerable it should ensure excellence and variety in provision. Providers should be judged by their performance and their performance alone. Unfortunately it is process rather than outcome that often decides which providers are favoured with state support. For instance, many Christian organisations that work in this area are denied public funding because of an ethos that guides their work – and their employment policies. This brings them into conflict with the equal opportunity policies of the state. In Scotland many of the major service providers are Christian, including the Church of Scotland Board of Social Responsibility, the Salvation Army, the Catholic Church and the Edinburgh and Glasgow City Missions. These organisations rightly feel that the services they provide would suffer if the people they employed did share the beliefs and aims of the organisation they are being paid to represent.

Bethany Christian Trust is an Edinburgh charity helping homeless and other vulnerable people overcome drug and alcohol addiction and re-enter mainstream society. Its inspirational founder and recently retired chief executive, Alan Berry, is certainly amongst the Christian heroes of contemporary Britain. From small beginnings in 1983, the trust now employs 79 staff and has an annual budget of nearly £2 million. In Edinburgh, statutory provision for drug addicts and homeless people is very patchy and disjointed. In contrast, Bethany offer seven progressive levels of care to clients from the most basic, providing food and shelter to rough sleepers, to the training, accommodation and support needed for people to re-enter the workplace. This system recognises and allows for failure; clients who relapse can access Bethany's services at a lower level before progressing up the ladder again. Relationships formed between Bethany staff and their clients are often sustained over months and years, providing the continuity and support that give recovering addicts a much better prospect of staying clean. Volunteers are used extensively and Bethany raise most of their funding themselves.

No one should be feel compelled to go to a religious organisation for help. There must always be a secular option. But as long as that choice does exist why shouldn't addicts turn to providers like Bethany if that is what they do choose? And why shouldn't state funding follow that choice if that is what is needed to make it available?

Conclusion

Few people would seriously pretend that Britain's drug policy doesn't need to change. Conservatives have a real opportunity to show not only that they can restore law and order to hard-pressed communities in places like Lambeth, but that they also have compassion for some of the most vulnerable people in our society. Our drug addicts need to be cared for. But it must be the kind of care that has the highest expectations of them as human beings, not as medical or criminal problems waiting to happen. If we really are serious about helping people to beat their addiction problems we need to do more than create thousands of methadone zombies. If even Labour has had enough of making people financially dependent on the state, why is it promoting policies to make them *chemically* dependent on the state? The good news is that there is an alternative. It can be seen in policies and programmes with a proven track record overseas and, in some cases, over here. It will take time, money and political will to make these available to everyone. But most of all it will take the belief that every person has dignity and potential.

1   www.thesite.org/info/drugs/drug_safety/reducing_the_risks.html, July 2002

2   *Hansard*, column 858, 12 June 2002

3   Ananova, 15 February 2002

4   Foreign Affairs, Council on Foreign Relations, May 1999.

5   Ibid.

6   D Tops; B Svensson; C Veldhoen, *The Drug Policies of Holland and Sweden: How Do They Compare?*, Director General of Research, European Parliament, 2001

7   Transform, the pro-liberalisation pressure group, puts it at 40, compared to 25 in the UK

8   Advisory Council on the Misuse of Drugs, *Reducing Drug Related Deaths*, 2000

9   For a comprehensive survey of the Swedish drug treatment system see D Tops; B Svensson; C Veldhoen, op. cit.

Two

Independence for those who can

Welfare systems can help people achieve independence for themselves and their families or can trap people in complex, often humiliating, mazes of dependency. A strong, prosperous economy may be able to afford to increase the number of people dependent upon state aid. But this only stores up trouble for inevitable periods of economic weakness. It's like building a house without a roof and hoping the sun will always shine. Sustainable welfare policy uses prosperity to invest in self-regenerating social institutions and values, helping people acquire the skills and relational networks necessary for independence.

Overleaf Cllr Sandy Bruce-Lockhart applies this principle to Kent County Council's supporting independence strategy.

Kent County Council's Supporting Independence strategy

Sandy Bruce-Lockhart

Sandy Bruce-Lockhart became Leader of Kent County Council in 1997 and has led the Kent Conservative Group at County Hall since 1993. A farmer by profession, Sandy farmed in Zimbabwe before settling in Kent, where he has farmed for thirty years with his wife and three children. Iain Duncan Smith and David Willetts have visited Kent to see and discuss Kent's groundbreaking Supporting Independence Programme.

The principles of independence, responsibility and freedom are at the heart of one nation conservatism. These principles are borne from our national characteristics of individualism and enterprise which throughout our long history have served the nation so well.

Sandy Bruce-Lockhart

Indeed, one wonders why it is that the British people, for centuries such splendid standard bearers of liberty, are now so meekly subdued by a centralising, controlling state. It is the growing, all-pervasive state and the intolerant new conformism of political correctness, which diminishes individuality, independence and enterprise. Conservatives must dismantle the growing state. We must deregulate business to allow enterprise to flourish, decentralise public services to foster the innovation and energy of those at the front line of delivery, and empower people to take responsibility for their own lives. Most importantly, in promoting independence, Conservatives must take, and hold, the centre ground on social issues.

In turning our principles into policy and action, one of our greatest challenges is to address and reduce the one-third of our population who now live dependent on some form of state benefit. The UK spends three times as much per head on social security expenditure as both the United States and Japan, and twice as much as Australia, Ireland and Canada.[1] Internationally we are high spenders on welfare, but low spenders, and ineffective on delivery, on the key preventative measures that are needed to tackle the root causes of social breakdown.

It is self-evident that we must reduce our welfare benefit bill and transfer this into preventative health, education and social programmes. Although the need to reduce benefit expenditure is clear in financial terms, for us the key drivers are greater social justice and the need to create a society which promotes independence, freedom and responsibility.

There are simply too many people who, through no fault of their own, find themselves trapped in dependency. In Kent we believe that by working with our partners across the public and voluntary sectors and by refocusing our services, we can help people to lift themselves out of dependency into independence, employment and more fulfilling lives, thus allowing them to take responsibility for themselves, their families and their future.

To address this challenge, Kent County Council has launched a major countywide project – the Supporting Independence Programme (SIP).[2] Together with the Treasury we have commissioned work from Oxford University to analyse welfare expenditure in Kent and our success in reducing it. It brings together the County Council with its local partners in the public, business and voluntary sectors and provides a 'noble goal' around which all are agreed.

Total public expenditure in Kent is £5.5 billion, of which some £2.5 billion is the government's social security expenditure.[3] Our Kent programme seeks to help people to free themselves from dependency and so reduce unnecessary expenditure on welfare – and in commitments already made by the Government, in a 'partnership agreement' with Kent, to re-invest part of these benefit savings back into public services and preventative programmes in the county.

The Kent Supporting Independence Programme
The Supporting Independence Programme has evolved from

the 'Kent Agreement', the county's Public Service Agreement with the government, a deal which promises freedoms and future financial reward for delivering jointly agreed local outcomes.

The Supporting Independence Programme consists of four strands of actions:

1   Analysing and monitoring welfare expenditure in Kent (being carried out by the Social Disadvantage Research Centre of the Department of Social Policy and Social Work at the University of Oxford).
2   Assessing all work, of KCC and its partners, which contributes to dependency reduction.
3   Refocusing the work of these partners in supporting independence projects.
4   Targeting specific projects in selected high-dependency wards.

The Nine Archetypes of Dependency

We have divided the categories of dependency into nine 'archetype' groups. These include lone parents, young teenage mums, young people leaving care and those with low educational attainment (including too many that have not had the education they deserve and whose interest in learning was never kindled). Then there are young adults who have never enjoyed a family upbringing, and people lost in what for them is a complex and highly confusing world. Talking to these groups, it is hard not to be affected by the depth of low self-esteem, loneliness and lack of purpose in their lives.

Our nine 'archetypes of dependency' are:

Young people
1   School leavers with low educational attainment
2   Youths with repeat youth offending records
3   In care / care leavers

Dependent adults
4   Lone parents
5   People lacking basis skills including life skills, social skills and those lacking low-level literacy or numeracy
6   People with alcohol or substance addictions
7   People with health problems, learning or physical disabilities on or applying for low-level long-term incapacity benefit
8   Transient or seasonal populations (including refugees, asylum seekers and homeless)
9   Long-term unemployed aged fifty plus

There are many reasons for dependency; some are natural circumstances like disability, where we are already providing real opportunities to work and trade, assisting disabled people into the independence they desire. However, we have looked carefully at the reasons for other forms of dependency – some of these are learnt, assimilated through deprived neighbourhoods, some are triggered by circumstances such as teenage pregnancy, school exclusion, criminal offending, domestic violence, redundancy and family breakdown. We have put in place projects which try to address each group. In many cases these are designed around individuals and groups of individuals, helping them and giving them the confidence to go through supported steps to take themselves out of dependency.

Across the county a great deal of work is already underway which supports the ambitions and targets of the SIP, particularly through the provision of mainstream services by local authorities, the police, the NHS and other public bodies. The emphasis is on action and on learning from the good practice already in place.

Major areas of work which are fundamental to the success of the SIP are discussed below.

Families first
The family is central to much of our work. The UK has amongst the worst rates in Europe for out-of-wedlock births, teenage pregnancy and family breakdown.[4] It is however the family which is the cornerstone of a civilised society. It is the family, with all its frailties and difficulties, but with its natural bonds and values that transcend generations, that makes sense of our lives. The family underpins order in our society – and gives us an ultimate purpose. Our Kent project recognises this and builds upon it.

There is such a thing as society

Our programmes started some three years ago with the introduction and expansion of our Family Centres. Often in the middle of deprived estates, these provide parenting courses for young mums and teach life courses and back-to-work skills. In deprived areas, the Council is placing teams of family support professionals into schools, in order to assist both children and parents. The refocusing of the long-term objective of children's services is centred around strengthening the family and has ensured a far more preventative approach and outlook to the delivery of services. Recent initiatives have already reduced the number of children being taken into care.

Equally with older people, we seek to assist them in continuing to live independent lives, ideally with their families in support. Rather than delivering purely reactive services, we are working to prevent people needing the services in the first place.

The best start in life

The quality of education plays a key role in determining levels of dependency and subsequent demand on services. A well-educated population is generally less deprived and potentially more independent. More importantly a higher general standard of education in traditionally deprived areas can help to make a real difference in terms of reversing the cycle of deprivation.

A common factor to many of the most deprived neighbourhoods is a lack of community spirit or social cohesion. Education is not purely about children being taught a curriculum at school, but instead should be taken in its widest possible sense, referring to a learning community. Schools can be the natural centres of many communities and lend themselves to much wider uses. Why should private pupils often have the opportunity to learn from eight o'clock in the morning to eight o'clock in the evening while state schoolchildren are turned out on to the streets at three every afternoon? Our project nicknamed 'The Schools that Never Sleep' extends the school day with breakfast clubs, homework clubs, holiday revision courses, sports and a variety of other clubs and activities. This also involves opening the school to the wider community during evenings, weekends and holidays for sport, recreation and learning, including parent and child IT courses and business start-up. As well as the social, community and educational benefits, extending the school day has a back-to-work benefit for parents.

Adult education is also of paramount importance in providing courses and skills training tailored for individuals. Kent already has twice the national average participation in adult education.[5] We are now trying to attract those people who can most benefit from these by moving to more socially acceptable 'learning gym' type courses, including those in east Kent held at the local football club, and in youth internet cafes with IT training rooms.

Real communities with shared values
Too many people live with an everyday fear of crime. This

restricts people's lives, particularly in hard-pressed neighbour-hoods. A loss of community spirit and identity, combined with high levels of transience within communities, has led to a breakdown in the social ties which have traditionally bound members of a neighbourhood together, and a consequent loss in order and purpose. Often this has alienated local people from the services that are there to help them. The reinforcement of order and the removal of lawlessness are prerequisites for supporting individuals, families and communities.

We are working closely with the Chief Constable and the Kent Police, recognising that some areas and groups are dispro-portionately involved in crime. We are employing an 'intelligence led' approach to place our staff and dedicated police officers into designated 'focus areas'. We are therefore targeting crime while pursuing preventative community-building through neighbourhood policing and activities for disaffected young people.

Each neighbourhood is different and requires a bespoke approach to capacity building. We are already making a differ-ence in the deprived areas of Kent through initiatives such as the 'Handy Van' Scheme, helping to secure the homes of the elderly and vulnerable. Our 'Community Wardens' scheme works in partnership with the police to give visible neighbour-hood policing, linking with local shops and businesses and other County Council services, such as local schools and youth groups.

At all times we are trying to build up local capacity and

strengthen neighbourhoods, empowering people rather than taking responsibilities from them.

A healthy community

Poor health is a major issue in deprived neighbourhoods where the incidence of disease, illness and long-term sickness and drug and alcohol abuse is high.

Investment in preventative health is key. Improving general levels of health, reducing teenage pregnancy and providing additional community-based preventative health services will help to reduce deprivation and improve general well-being, while decreasing pressure on acute hospital services. Our actions promote healthy living for all ages and create new initiatives for sport, exercise and a variety of activities, as well as promoting improved nutrition.

Supporting Independence Projects

The Kent Programme also launches a series of high-intensity Supporting Independence Projects in priority neighbourhoods. These take the form of targeted education, social care, health or community safety interventions in 25 county wards where there is a high level of dependence.

Fifteen Kent wards are in the ten per cent most deprived wards in England and Wales as measured in terms of the Index of Multiple Deprivation (IMD),[6] a ranking which assesses six different aspects of deprivation – income, employment, health and disability, education, housing and access to services. The local community must be at the heart of decision-making and involved directly in the delivery of these projects.

Conclusion

Four years ago, we published the Kent County Council core policy statement – stating that our Conservative County Council 'has a role in creating a society with a sense of purpose, community, order and belonging'. We have now added to this the Kent Supporting Independence Programme, an ambitious initiative launched by the County Council with the support of all major public agencies in the county together with businesses, voluntary organisations and many local community groups. We know the aims of our work are challenging, but we all share the determination to succeed in reversing the spiral of deprivation, family breakdown and dependency on the state. Conservatives must strive for others to enjoy the true independence that so many of us are fortunate enough to take for granted.

---

1   Based upon *The Changing Welfare State – Social Security Funding*, Department of Social Security, 2000
2   Kent Supporting Independence Programme, 2002
3   Estimated public revenue expenditure by district for the KCC area, 2001/02
4   Office of National Statistics, *Social Trends 2002* (Out-of-Wedlock Births); Social Exclusion Unit, *Teenage Pregnancy*, June 1999 (Teenage Pregnancy); *Eurostat Yearbook*, 2001 (Family Breakdown)

Sandy Bruce-Lockhart

5 Figures from KCC Adult Education, 2000

6 Department of Environment, Transport and the Regions, *Index of Multiple Deprivation*, 2001

Three

And security for those who can't

Many vulnerable people – perhaps because of age or serious disability – will always need special care and support. Compassionate Conservatives in government will guarantee a financial safety-net for vulnerable people. This will be particularly generous for those people who cannot support themselves.

Overleaf Nicholas Hillman applies this principle to support for older pensioners.

Tackling pensioner poverty

Nicholas Hillman

Previously a teacher, Nicholas Hillman now works for the Shadow Secretary of State for Work and Pensions, David Willetts, with whom he has co-authored pamphlets on the benefits trap and helping lone parents. He has also worked on voluntary projects in Africa, South America and Eastern Europe.

Conservatives believe in independence for those who can work not just because we support economic efficiency, but also because we believe in human dignity. The same principle shapes our views on the help that should be offered to people who are unable to work. A simple functional case could be made in favour of cash handouts from the state for those in need, but there are problems with such a crude approach. As well as ignoring the desirable incentives for those that are able to work, such a mechanistic view takes little regard of the dignity owed to those that cannot work. When contemplating social security reform, we must remember what is right in principle, and not just what offers short-term relief.

The Prime Minister's target of eradicating child poverty by the end of the next decade has moved the spotlight away from poverty amongst other groups. This is a great pity because there are millions of other people who are also forced to survive on very low incomes. For example, two million pensioners have incomes that are below sixty per cent of median income and the figure is the same as it was in 1996/7.[1]

Pensioner poverty today

Many pensioners live in comparative comfort. For example, the mean income of the richest fifth of pensioner couples is £786 a week or over £40,000 a year. The age group that, back in the 1950s, provided the first real market for products aimed at teenagers is now the focus of a new market aimed specifically at wealthier older people. But this welcome development cannot conceal the real deprivation faced by millions of others of a similar age.

Some people have little idea what it means to be poor in modern Britain, but the figures are all too clear. The median net income of the poorest twenty per cent of single pensioners is just £65 a week once housing costs have been taken into account. And some groups are much worse off than others: the average gross income of single female pensioners is over £40 a week lower than for single male pensioners; and the average gross income of couples in which the head of the household is over 75 is £80 a week less than for recently retired pensioner couples.

Furthermore, there has been no recent improvement in the position of older people compared with other groups in society. The proportion of pensioners in the bottom fifth of the total income distribution, before housing costs, fell from 47 per cent to 25 per cent between 1979 and 1994/5. Since then, it has remained unchanged and has even grown slightly on the after-housing-costs measure.[2]

It is not only crude financial measurements that reflect the vulnerability of many pensioners. A recent television documentary featured a 77-year-old widower who has been unable to lock his flat since the children who regularly break in smashed the frame of his front door. The man is so ashamed of his situation that he does not want his two sons to know when he dies. The same programme also featured a disabled 71-year-old woman who has been on and off the streets for twenty years and who currently sleeps outside propped up in a wheelchair.[3]

There is a common view that if pensioner poverty exists at all, then it will disappear in the near future. A recent newspaper article, for example, berated 'the tendency still to mention pensions and poverty in the same breath'.[4] But it is wrong to assume that the passage of time ensures an ever higher income for people in their retirement. Indeed, there are worthwhile grounds to believe the opposite could be true in the future. Increasing longevity, the closure of the majority of final salary pension schemes to new members and changes in the labour market are just some of the reasons why we cannot simply expect pensioner incomes to grow inexorably.

Our duty towards pensioners who are in need extends beyond a vague sense of charity. It is not just that older people helped to build and shape modern Britain when they were younger, they are also playing an increasingly important role in the maintenance of civil society today. The level of volunteering amongst people aged 65 and over is rising fast, whereas it is falling for all other age groups, and it would almost certainly increase further still if pensioners had more economic security.[5] Moreover, the atomisation of society has led to an increase, rather than a fall, in the importance of grandparenting: 'It is possible that present changes in our society are so fundamental that they are leading towards new equations of mutual support in family life, in which (some) grandparents could recover a central place.'[6] These facts might help to explain why a majority of people believe that pensions should be the priority for any extra spending on social benefits and why 96 per cent of respondents think it is 'definitely' or 'probably' the government's responsibility to provide a decent standard of living for older people.[7]

The Labour Government may be sincere in their desire to help both current and future pensioners, but their polices are proving to be counter productive. The various reforms are hugely complicated, but the problems they raise are clear. The enormous extension of means testing through the Minimum Income Guarantee and the forthcoming Pension Credit is taking away much of the rationale for both the State Second Pension and stakeholder pensions, whilst also undermining people's ability to be independent in their retirement. As one commentator has written, 'it seems obtuse to structure a pension system with built in, long-term, obsolescence.'[8]

Labour's reforms to the *delivery* of benefits for pensioners are also a cause for concern. The new Pension Service is designed to allow pensioners to get 'all their benefit help from one single, accessible point – that may be by telephone, post or the internet.'[9] But in reality it is likely to spread feelings of isolation. There will be no Pension Service call centre in London or the South East and the poorest pensioners, who have the most contact with the benefits system, are not going to access the web to claim their benefits – internet users tend to be younger, richer and more highly educated than non-users and they include only five per cent of people aged over 65.[10] What is more, the new Pension Service will rely initially on the old DSS computer system, which in the words of the former Secretary of State for Work and Pensions is 'very decrepit'.[11]

Targeting pensioner poverty

The problems of widespread pensioner poverty thus pose a real challenge, but they are not insurmountable. The Conservative response should lie in strengthening those existing institutions and policy levers that work and reforming the parts of the system that are keeping so many pensioners in deprivation. The rest of this chapter examines the action that central government could take to improve pensioners' incomes. But that is obviously not the whole story. As explained elsewhere in this book, if the lives of Britain's poorest people are to be transformed, such changes need to be complemented by a renaissance in the institutions that stand between the individual and the state, as well as by radical reform of the public services.

The basic state pension is as popular as any state benefit is ever likely to be. Its take-up is almost universal, with 98 per cent of pensioners in receipt,[12] and it is subject to very little fraud. Yet the current Government have downgraded it relentlessly in favour of additional means testing: although income-related help for pensioners has traditionally been set at a similar level to the basic pension, the Minimum Income Guarantee is now worth thirty per cent more; around two-thirds of pensioners could eventually be eligible for the fiendishly complicated Pension Credit; and Child Dependency Increases, which are as old as the basic state pension itself, are about to be replaced for new pensioners by the means-tested Child Tax Credit.

This strategy is neither successful nor popular: the proportion of pensioners taking up their means-tested entitlement is falling[13] and, according to the Social Attitudes Survey, 83 per cent of people now consider the state pension to be 'very low' or 'a bit on the low side'.[14] In short, Labour's changes to state benefits for pensioners have been in exactly the wrong direction.

Nonetheless, no government is ever likely to have sufficient resources to provide a very large increase in the basic state pension for all pensioners, particularly now that the number of older people is growing so rapidly. The solution must therefore lie in targeting resources more accurately. Older pensioners are more likely to be living in poverty than their younger counterparts. Sir Keith Joseph understood this when he awarded a larger increase in the basic state pension for all those aged over eighty in 1971,[15] but unfortunately – like the £10 Christmas Bonus introduced in the following year – the Age Addition is still set at its original level (25 pence a week), which is now derisory.

It is for these reasons that the Conservative front bench were right to try and amend the recent State Pension Credit Bill so that the billions of pounds that are due to be spent on the new measure would instead have gone on a higher basic state pension for older pensioners. We should now continue to build a cross-party and extra-parliamentary consensus that backs extra help for those pensioners who have high needs, but no realistic expectation of increasing their income by their own efforts, and which avoids the pitfalls of additional means testing.

Improving the state pension

We should also look at other ways of improving the state pension. At the moment, pensioners receive a mixture of the Winter Fuel Payment, the Christmas Bonus, a Concessionary TV licence and the Age Addition on top of their contributory, means-tested and disability benefits. Apart from the 'free' TV licence, there is no legislative provision for any of these measures to be increased each year, even in line with price inflation, and many pensioners find them a confusing jumble. Some of these extra payments are more popular than others and no Government would wish to abolish any of them without an equally or more generous alternative in place, but some rationalisation would undoubtedly be worthwhile. The key could lie in holding an informed debate about the proportion of our national wealth that should be spent on pensioners' benefits. If such a discussion was started, it would be much easier to make suggestions about the best way to deliver this support, and unscrupulous politicians in other parties would find it less easy to run scare stories about the abolition of particular benefits.

Other elements of state provision for pensioners also need to be improved, particularly those measures which are aimed at the most vulnerable people of all, such as the Social Fund and Attendance Allowance. The Government's response to the report on the Social Fund by the Social Security Select Committee was very disappointing in its lack of imagination[16] and it is likely that pensioners will find access to the Fund even more difficult now that the Pension Service is up and running. This is because their only access to it will be through Jobcentre Plus offices, with which they are generally expected to have no contact.

Ministers have been similarly complacent with regard to benefits for people with disabilities. For example, whilst the Disability Living Allowance Mobility Component has been extended to three- and four-year-olds, almost nothing has been done to improve the transport needs of older disabled people, such as those who claim Attendance Allowance.

Preparing for the future

Even with reform, however, the current framework of state provision will never be able to provide a comfortable retirement for the majority of people. That is why Conservatives should also seek ways to increase private saving. This too is in line with our past traditions. The original pamphlet from the One Nation Group, which was published in 1950 and includes contributions from Edward Heath, Iain Macleod and Enoch Powell, remains relevant today: 'every possible encouragement must be given to individual provision against old age. The instinct to save for the future is no doubt as strong as it has ever been; it is therefore peculiarly unfortunate, when the need for saving is greater than ever, that a Socialist Government should put so many obstacles in its way.'[17] The pamphlet also calls for more flexibility with regard to the age of retirement and notes that older people are sometimes more reliable employees than younger workers.

The One Nation Group's three objectives – more saving, an end to the gulf between work and retirement and less discrimination by employers on grounds of age – are perhaps even more relevant today than they were in the 1950s, when funded pension coverage was growing rapidly and life expectancy was much lower. Yet Labour's policies are moving away from such aims. For example, the new State Pension Credit will increase the marginal tax and benefit withdrawal rates of many pensioners, thereby discouraging them from continuing to work.

Funded pensions are often regarded as the great welfare success of the last century, but their coverage is now declining.[18] Firm action needs to be taken soon if this change is to be reversed. Conservatives have done their best to mitigate the problem: David Curry's Private Member's Bill on annuity reform has led to a number of parliamentary defeats for the Government; pressure from David Willetts has helped to delay the implementation of the controversial accounting standard FRS17; and Tory peers persuaded the Government to give way on concurrency. But these modest victories need to be followed up. We now need to co-operate fully with ministers and the pensions industry on reducing red tape where this makes sense, to challenge the view that people regard pension saving as a tax fiddle and to put forward radical ideas on how to incentivise younger workers to save.

Ending age discrimination

Many people consider the state pension age, which is currently 60 for women and 65 for men, to be too low. But whilst the Government probably have been overly reluctant to contribute to this debate, it is something of a red herring. The most pressing problem is the age at which people leave their last paid job – at the moment, only 39 per cent of men and 47 per cent of women are in work in the year before they reach state pension age[19] and there is evidence to suggest that, for men at least, the figure could fall further in the future.[20] As the Institute for Employment Studies has pointed out, inactivity amongst older people 'is often greatly resented by those experiencing it, and it represents a major contribution to poverty in later life'.[21]

Whilst ministers might speak about ending 'the sheer cliff edge between work and retirement',[22] they have failed to give a lead in practice. The normal retirement age for senior civil servants, including those in the Department for Work and Pensions, remains at sixty and irreplaceable experts within the public sector, such as the heart surgeon Sir Magdi Yacoub, are still forced to retire against their will. Moreover, even though the Performance and Innovation Unit called over two and a half years ago for a review of the rule which stops someone from receiving their company pension whilst staying with the same employer, the regulation remains in force.[23] This means that older people who wish to gradually divorce themselves from the labour market have to leave their existing employer to do so.

The Government's lackadaisical approach is perhaps most obvious with regard to legislation on age discrimination in employment. When in opposition, Ian McCartney, the current Minister for Pensions, told the House of Commons 'an incoming Labour Government will introduce comprehensive legislation to make age discrimination in employment illegal'.[24] After winning office, Labour instead chose to publish a Code of Practice, which has had almost no impact – just two per cent of companies have changed their approach as a result of the Code's publication.[25] Whilst a few firms have put in place innovative flexible retirement policies, such schemes are conspicuous by their rarity and have little to do with Government action.[26]

Some Conservatives might instinctively dislike the idea of yet more burdens on employers in the form of new age discrimination rules. Yet there are good grounds for thinking that we should take the initiative in this area. First, the current system is not working. Secondly, such action would undoubtedly be popular – around ninety per cent of people aged between 50 and 69 think employers discriminate against older workers[27] and the figure is also high amongst other age groups.[28] Thirdly, Britain is obliged by a European Commission Directive to implement age discrimination legislation by December 2006. Fourthly, unlike most business regulation, the change is expected to bring net cash benefits to firms.[29] And fifthly, the international experience in countries such as the United States suggests there are many advantages in having such legislation.

My personal view is that Conservatives should consider whether to press the Government to implement the European Directive earlier than 2006. At the same time, we should not feel obliged to back any decisions Labour take on how to implement the Directive.

It would make sense to link support for early age discrimination legislation to other changes that help people stay in work. There are 1.2 million Incapacity Benefit claimants aged between 50 and state pension age[30] and we should commit ourselves to making it easier for people with disabilities to work, possibly by revisiting the imaginative proposal in the 2001 General Election manifesto to establish an Incapacity Benefit fundholder. The regime for deferring the basic state pension is also crying out for improvement.

Conclusion

Additional support for older pensioners and other reforms to the basic state pension, improvements to the Social Fund and Attendance Allowance, new incentives to save for retirement, backing for age discrimination legislation and extra help for people with disabilities who wish to work compose a coherent, forward looking and eminently Conservative programme to ease the problems faced by vulnerable older people. But such a series of policies must not become a cynical ploy for winning votes. Older people are shrewd enough to see straight through such an unworthy tactic. A desire to ease the problems faced by the least fortunate members of our society and to restore their dignity should not only be one of the means of gaining office, it must also be one of the central reasons why we seek office in the first place.

1   Office of National Statistics, *Households Below Average Income 1994/5–2000/01*, 2002, page 129

2   Figures from the Office of National Statistics, The Pensioners' Incomes Series 2000/01, 2002

3   True Vision, *Old*, transmitted on Channel 4, 13 May 2002

4   Andrew Alexander, 'Beware of myths becoming history', *Daily Mail*, 14 June 2002

5   Justin Davis Smith, *The 1997 National Survey of Volunteering*, 1998, pages 26-30

6   Geoff Dench, Jim Ogg and Katarina Thomson, *The role of grandparents*, British Social Attitudes, 1999, page 153

7   John Hills, *Following or leading public opinion?: Policy, poverty, social security and public attitudes since 1997*, Institute for Fiscal Studies, 2002, page 3 and page 11; John Hills, *Poverty and social security: What rights? Whose responsibilities?*, British Social Attitudes, 2001, pages 16-17

8   Deborah Cooper, 'A new contract for welfare: partnership in pensions', *Economic Affairs*, volume 19, number 3, 1999, page

9   Alistair Darling quoted in 'New Names – New Start: Government Steps up High Street' Services, Department for Work and Pensions, 2 April 2001

10   Jonathan Gardner and Andrew Oswald, 'Internet use: the digital divide', *British Social Attitudes*, 2001, page 163; see also Office of National Statistics, 'Internet access:

Nicholas Hillman

Households and Individuals', 2 July 2002

11   Alistair Darling, Work and Pensions Select Committee, *Pension Credit*, volume 2, 2002, Q208 and Q224

12   Office of National Statistics, *The Pensioners' Incomes Series 2000/01*, 2002, page 47, table 8

13   Office of National Statistics, *Income Related Benefits: Estimates of Take-Up in 1999/2000* 2001, pages 15, 25 and 31

14   John Hills, 'Poverty and social security: What rights? Whose responsibilities?', *British Social Attitudes*, 2001, page 17

15   Keith Joseph, *Hansard*, column 1500, 31 March 1971

16   Department for Work and Pensions, Report on the Social Fund, 2001

17   Iain Macleod and Angus Maude (eds), *One Nation: A Tory Approach to Social Problems*, 1950, pages 64-66

18   This fall is tracked in chapter 7 of the annual *Family Resources Survey* published by the Office of National Statistics

19   Ruth Kelly, *Hansard*, column 1055W, 27 June 2002

20   Catherine Barham, 'Patterns of economic inactivity among older men', *Labour Market Trends*, volume 110, number. 6, 2002, pages 301-309

21   The Institute for Employment Studies, *Evaluation of the New Deal 50 plus: Research with individuals (Wave 2)*, 2001, page 2

22   Andrew Smith quoted in Department for Work and Pensions press release, 'Smith calls for end of cliff edge between work and retirement', 20 June 2002

23   Performance and Innovation Unit, *Winning the Generation Game: Improving opportunities for people aged 50-65 in work and community activity*, 2000, page 75

24   Ian McCartney, Hansard, column 618, 9 February 1996

25   Department for Work and Pensions, *Evaluation of the Code of Practice on Age Diversity in Employment: Report of Research Findings*, 2001, table 8.11, page 166

26   Department for Work and Pensions, *Flexible Retirement: A Snapshot of Large Employers' Initiatives*, 2002

27   Department for Work and Pensions, *Evaluation of the Code of Practice on Age Diversity in Employment: Report of Research Findings*, 2001, page 118

28   Age Concern, *Age Today,* issue 1, 2002, pages 12–13

29   Department of Trade and Industry, *Detailed Regulatory Impact Assessment*, 2001

30   Office of National Statistics, *Incapacity Benefit and Severe Disablement Allowance: Quarterly Summary Statistics*, 2002, page 12 and page 15

Four

Successful social inclusion requires courage and honesty about family life

Any society that is genuinely committed to social justice will value the family. It is difficult to envisage a renewal of Britain's poorest communities without greater recognition of the importance of parenthood and the family. Members of a free society should be able to choose their own family arrangements but public policy should recognise and encourage those choices that most benefit children and the nation as a whole.

Overleaf Jill Kirby applies this principle to government policy and the institution of marriage.

How will we respond to the evidence for marriage?

Jill Kirby

Jill Kirby is a lawyer turned full-time mother who writes and broad-casts on family issues. Jill chairs the family policy committee of the Centre for Policy Studies and is a consultant to Renewing One Nation, the social affairs unit at Conservative Central Office. She lives in south London with her husband and three sons.

The family is the heart of society. It is the first, crucial, example of our human need for co-operation and interdependence; the unit which is always more than the sum of its parts. Most important of all, the family provides protection and security for humanity at its most vulnerable and dependent: in infancy and early childhood.

This far, the consensus still holds, because everyone accepts that children need families. Indeed, almost every politician can agree that supporting and strengthening family life are desirable goals. But the methods for achieving those goals present a much greater challenge, and there are two reasons for this. The first is the problem of definition – there is today very little consensus about what defines 'a family'. The second is the problem of truth – the importance of telling the truth about family structure and the dangerous Orwellian impetus to conceal it.

Families versus relationships

Less than five years ago, in his enthusiasm to embrace a New Labour vision for Britain, Tony Blair expressed his determination to scrutinise every area of policy for its impact on family life. His Government issued a consultation paper which described marriage as 'the surest foundation for raising children'.[1] It all seemed promising, but the confidence of those early days soon melted away.

By the spring of 2002 the picture was very different. The Ministerial Group on the Family had been closed down, replaced by a Cabinet sub-committee whose chairman, David Blunkett, reportedly agreed 'not to re-open the debate on the subject of marriage and family structure'.[2] The Government decided to support an amendment to its Adoption Bill which would enable cohabiting couples to adopt children jointly. It also withdrew funding for National Marriage Week. The Lord Chancellor's Department issued a report on marriage and relationship support which declared, in a curious rewriting of a familiar expression: 'the adult couple is the cornerstone of the family.' In the words of Lord Irvine, in his introduction to that report, 'supporting adult couple relationships is a vital and growing part of the Government's wider agenda for supporting families'.[3]

So there we have it. The Government's new definition of family is based on 'adult couple relationships'. Imagine asking a group of teenagers about their lifetime aspirations, and receiving this response – 'My dream is to have an adult couple relationship and two children.' But the Lord Chancellor is not joking, so it is worth asking: What does this new definition actually mean? What is an 'adult couple relationship'?

First, two positive aspects. The word 'adult' does seem to rule out under-age sexual relationships, and the word 'couple' seems to acknowledge that a child ideally needs two parents. But it carefully avoids questions of gender, thus neatly encompassing same-sex relationships. And by failing to allude to marriage, the definition also sidesteps the question of exclusivity or commitment, and this is for a reason. There is, of course, a massive difference between a 'relationship' and a 'family'. 'Relationships' are important to everyone. Plainly it is good to have friends, to enjoy the company of others, or indeed of one special person. Relationships are like friendships, they may last for a few weeks or they may be lifelong; they may involve just two people or a whole crowd. But a relationship does not carry a special and exclusive status, it does not involve a pledge or a public sign of commitment. Relationships, like friendships, can be rewarding for a time and then can cool off; at different times in our lives different friends are important to us. But families are more than friendships, and family life is much more than a set of relationships.

130

This is where the new definitions let us down. Because in true New Labour fashion, the desire to please everyone has resulted in meaningless statements that cover any and every aspect of human contact, but do nothing to support or strengthen family life. Crucially, they fail to give any signals about protecting children. As Iain Duncan Smith pointed out at the time of the adoption debate, cohabiting couples are much more likely to split up than married couples, and this is so particularly when they have children. Data shows that only eight per cent of married couples break up before their child is five, but 52 per cent of cohabiting parents have parted by then.[4] So that inviting an unmarried couple, who have taken the decision not to marry, to take joint responsibility for a child who has been in care is much riskier than giving the responsibility to a married couple.

In the words of Paul Boateng: 'We know that cohabitation is less likely to inculcate stability in a family than marriage. But that is not making a moral judgment. It is just a fact.'[5] It is, however, an uncomfortable fact for the Government to accept, and one which most of Mr Boateng's colleagues find very hard to state.

The M word

The reason why the new definitions of the family have come about is that this Government, in common with so many policy advisers, academics, charities and journalists, has become frightened of the 'M word'. Because pre-marital cohabitation is widespread, and because forty per cent of children are now born outside marriage, it is commonly assumed that to indicate support for marriage would offend a large section of society. In fact, much of that fear is unfounded – many cohabitees still aspire to marriage, and many lone parents hope that their children will marry before having families of their own.

Most significantly, however, failure to talk about the value of marriage has fuelled its decline. Through fear of offending, the Government has not just failed in its duty to support the real cornerstone of society, it has actively contributed to its erosion by withdrawing fiscal recognition for marriage, and in building welfare policies which impose substantial financial penalties on it.[6] Of course, there is disagreement over the extent to which financial considerations affect a couple's decision. But whatever the impact, it will be felt most heavily amongst lower-income groups – where marriage rates are the lowest. Furthermore, in disadvantaging marriage the Government is sending a negative signal about the value of marriage to individuals and to society. Given the wealth of evidence that marriage is associated with positive outcomes for both individuals and society, that signal is not only negative, but also dishonest.

Politicians also need to ask themselves if it is solely the case that people shape institutions, or is it also true that institutions shape people? The presence of commitment between adults is signalled by their decision to enter into a public contract, namely marriage, but the presence of that contract also then enhances their sense of commitment. Where this commitment precedes the birth of children, parents are much less likely to split up, as the data shows. So the public bond not only strengthens the parental relationship, but also increases the commitment to the children. Even where the married parents end up divorced, research shows that the non-custodial parent is more likely to remain in regular contact with the child, and to pay maintenance, than the separated cohabitee.[7]

Marriage has a further role in shaping interaction because it enables a couple to invest more heavily in each other and in the future of their relationship, thereby increasing the likelihood of its longevity – it is a virtuous circle. Interdependence is a crucial factor in the success of a relationship, especially when children enter the equation. On the arrival of a child one spouse (still very often the mother) will become partly, or sometimes wholly, dependent on the other for financial support during the child's early years. She will also be heavily dependent for moral support and loving care from the child's father in ways that will require from him some sacrifice of personal freedom and independent decision-making.

The two most significant qualities that define a family, and which most clearly distinguish it from relationships in general, are surely commitment and interdependence. These two distinguishing features are not simply coincidental to marriage; they flow from the institution itself, and their presence is the main reason why the institution of marriage can truly be described as 'the surest foundation for raising children'.

Next, let us consider why children need that sure foundation.

What about the children?
More children than ever before in our history are witnessing the separation of their parents, whether through divorce or the

breakdown of cohabiting relationships. So there is no shortage of evidence about the outcomes of such separation. It is estimated that more than twenty per cent of all first-time mothers have separated from the father of their child by the time their baby is a year old[8] – so the child's earliest experiences will be clouded by unhappiness and loss. Around a quarter of children in Britain are now living in one-parent households,[9] nearly all of these headed by a mother alone, struggling to provide the love and security which her children need. This is way ahead of the European average, and nearly twice the number of such households in France and Germany.[10]

At the same time, an ever-increasing mass of data shows that children raised outside married families can be at a real disadvantage; from babyhood onwards. Infant deaths are substantially higher for children of lone or cohabiting parents than married parents. The UK has the highest teenage birth rate in Europe, by a wide margin, and babies born to teenage mothers are sixty per cent more likely to die in their first year.[11] Children brought up outside marriage are at higher risk of accidents and physical abuse; they are twice as likely to have mental health problems than the children of married couples, to perform less well in school, become sexually active at a younger age, suffer depression and turn to drugs, smoking and heavy drinking. They are also more likely to become teenage mothers and to experience the breakdown of their own relationships.[12] Not only are these children vulnerable, unhappy and poor, they are also the children most likely to be caught up in crime from an early age. A series of both US and UK studies shows a steady connection between broken homes and delinquency.[13] The rapidly rising rates of youth crime in this country demonstrate the costly and damaging consequences of our failure to raise children in stable families.

So perhaps it should be more widely recognised that children pay a high price for the freedom of adults. If we are truly to exercise compassion, adult choice may sometimes have to be limited by duties to the vulnerable. As American sociologist Barbara Dafoe Whitehead points out:

> In a culture of divorce, children are the most "unfree". Divorce abrogates children's rights to be reasonably free from adult cares and woes, to enjoy the association of both parents on a daily basis, to remain innocent of the social services and therapy, and to spend family time in ways that are not dictated by the courts ... Divorce involves a radical redistribution of hardship, from adults to children, and therefore cannot be viewed as a morally neutral act.[14]

The widespread and convenient belief that parental divorce and separation are 'morally neutral' is rarely challenged. Yet Dafoe's thesis is palpably right. Adult preferences are the reason for separation, yet if there are children involved, it is they who suffer the most disruption and the long-term consequences. As Michelle Elliott of UK charity Kidscape said recently: 'Excluding cases where there has been violence, most children from broken homes would give anything to see their parents back together.'[15]

In a society which is allegedly child-centred, why is there so much importance attached to the freedom of adults, and so little thought given to the consequences for children?

Hiding the truth

Since marriage is so important and its benefits to children so clear, it seems surprising that this vital institution has been so neglected and that there is such reluctance to speak the truth about marriage. The widespread use of a whole new vocabulary of family life plays a significant part here. The Lord Chancellor's 'adult couple relationship' is just one example of the new terminology. The all-purpose word 'partner' has nowadays largely overtaken the words 'husband' and 'wife'. Mothers and fathers have, officially, become 'parents and caregivers'. Step-families are now described as 'reconstituted' or 'blended' families. Where children are living with their own two married parents, they will generally be included in the catch-all description 'couple families'. This new language pervades most official documentation, from guidelines for education or social services to government consultations and reports.

There are two dangers in using this new vocabulary to mask reality. The first is that the new language does not merely reflect a new way of living, it helps to bring it about. Anyone familiar with the works of George Orwell will acknowledge that language is an important tool for those who wish to change society – and for helping people forget the past. Abandoning the titles of husband and wife in favour of the all-purpose 'partner' contributes to the decline of the institution of marriage itself. The use of 'parents and caregivers' denies to mothers and fathers the importance of their special and different roles in the lives of their children, and helps to make one or other of those roles expendable. Describing a step-family as 'blended' implies a degree of smooth acceptance which ignores the pain experienced by a child who has lost a much-loved mother or father and has been obliged – often in the interests of adult convenience – to accept a substitute.

The second danger in obscuring the truth is that important information ceases to be available. Use of terms like 'couple families' does not distinguish between married, cohabiting and step families. In assessing data provided by the agencies of government, how are we to draw any conclusions on the impact of changes in family life, if we cannot get hold of the facts? *Social Trends*, the annual reference work on UK society published by the Office of National Statistics, features in its 2002 edition a special section on children. Intended to 'present an overview of social trends since the early 1980s that have impacted on children', the section provides detailed summaries from a range of sources on education, child health, family formation and so on. But a key chart which accompanies the section, showing 'families with dependent children by family type', divides families into just three categories: lone mother, lone father and 'married/cohabiting couple'. Surely a distinction between married and cohabiting couples would be helpful to every user of the book?

Government agencies are not alone in such practices. A major report on child homelessness was published last year by The Children's Society (a Church of England charity). The report contained some shocking statistics about children who run away from home. It showed that children living in step-families are three times as likely to run away from home as those from two-parent families, and children of lone parents are twice as likely to do so.[16] But the definition given for 'two-parent family' was 'where the young person is living with both birth or adoptive parents'. There was no mention of the M word.

One of the few other nations rivalling the UK in the family breakdown stakes is the US, where misinformation through catch-all language is also prevalent. Earlier this year the *New York Times* carried an item headlined 'Two parents not always best for children, study finds'. The implication was that research had emerged which was critical of the traditional family. In fact, the study showed that children whose mothers acquired new live-in boyfriends after a break-up were at greater risk than those whose mothers remained single. This research was consistent with plenty of other data showing that children tend to be safer and healthier in a lone-mother home than with a step-father, especially where the step-father is not married to the child's mother. Likewise, a report from the US Centers for Disease Control claimed six per cent of all pregnant women are battered by their 'husbands or partners'. But analysis showed that for every pregnant married woman beaten by her husband, four unmarried pregnant women were beaten by boyfriends. Marriage is the strongest predictor of low rates of abuse in the home – stronger than race, age, housing conditions or educational attainment.[17] Partial information based on 'partnering' and 'parenting' disguises the significance of marriage as a key institution for protecting vulnerable people.

It doesn't have to be like this

So what is the role of the state and of society in upholding and promoting family stability? How should politicians respond to the evidence that marriage does still matter? The present Government appears to believe that it can be 'neutral' on the subject. But in applying a tax and welfare regime that actually penalises marriage, and by stifling the truth about the link between marriage and family stability, it is not being neutral. It is promoting an anti-marriage society.

There are several options for government action all of which are compatible with, and even essential to, the ideal of a tolerant and compassionate society. First of all, taxation and welfare should be reformed to remove disincentives to getting married. The Government need not look far for a better model. Most other European economies retain tax and benefit systems built around marriage. By contrast, families in Britain suffer a 'double whammy': taxation is based on individual assessment with no allowance for marriage, yet benefit entitlement is jointly assessed, carrying penalties of as much as £70 per week for marriage or open cohabitation.[18] This is plainly wrong, not only in terms of the signals it provides but also because such penalties hurt people on the lowest incomes most of all. How can a society that leaves such stumbling stones in the path of vulnerable people be described as tolerant?

Secondly, government and the agencies of the state could be more supportive to people who want to get married. Public funds are routinely used for a huge range of family and parenting courses, so why shouldn't these include marriage education and support? In both the US and Australia, such programmes receive substantial government funding, and are seen as an important tool not just in restoring the significance of marriage but also in improving marital stability.

In Britain in 2002, however, the prospects of reform seem remote, because ministers are still choking on the M word. What is their problem? As journalist Anne McElvoy points out:

> the consequences of more and more children growing up in fatherless households are all around us and it is the poor who suffer most from social breakdown and its consequences. Someone has to break the mindless taboo which says this can't be addressed.[19]

It would, surely, be quite reasonable for the Government to break the taboo by declaring: 'We recognise that, whether intentionally or not, we have failed to uphold the married family and that our policies have sometimes actively discouraged it. We accept that the decision whether or not to marry is a private one. But since it is clear that marriage is most conducive to lasting relationships and to the welfare of children, we believe that it should be supported and that couples wishing to marry should receive every encouragement. We therefore propose changes to the welfare regime which will remove the marriage penalty and we will examine taxation, education and housing policies with the object of encouraging marriage and committed parenting.'

Is that really so very difficult to say?

1   *Supporting Families*, Home Office, 1998

2   'Marriage too risky for Cabinet support', *Daily Telegraph*, 11 March 2002

3   *Moving Forward Together*, Lord Chancellor's Department 2002

4   Kiernan, K., 'Childbearing outside Marriage in Western Europe', *Population Trends*, 1999

5   Family in Crisis conference, 14 September 1998

6   *The Lone Parent Trap*, Civitas, 2002

7   Morgan, P., 'Marriage-Lite: the Rise of Cohabitation and its Consequences', Civitas, 2000

8   Pankhurst, L., *Early Days – a strategy for early intervention and prevention*, Child Psychotherapy Trust, 2000

9   *Social Trends 2002*, The Stationery Office

10   Eurostat 2001

11   See the author's paper *Broken Hearts*, Centre for Policy Studies, 2002

12   Rodgers, B. & Prior, J., *Divorce and Separation: The Outcomes for Children*, Joseph Rowntree Foundation, 1998

13   See for example, Wadsworth, M., *National Survey of Health and Development* 1946 cohort', 1979; Kolvin et al., *Newcastle 1,000 Family Study*, 1990; Farrington & West, *Cambridge Study in Delinquent Development*, 1990; Farrington, *Understanding and Preventing Youth Crime*, Joseph Rowntree Foundation, 1996.

14   Whitehead, B., *The Divorce Culture*, 1997

15   'Why we are the divorce capital of Europe', The Mirror, 12 February 2002

16   *Home Run: Families and Young Runaways'* The Children's Society, October 2001

17   Leo, J., 'Ignoring the Churn Factor', www.uexpress.com, 2002

18   'The Lone Parent Trap', op. cit.

19   *Evening Standard*, 5 June 2002

Five

3D care in a 3D world

Poverty in Britain was once primarily material in character. Strong families and communities tended to help people cope with shortages of income. Today, people have higher incomes but this material wealth cannot compensate for the new fragility of public order and of family and community life. Neither a bigger state nor market forces can replace the holistic care provided through social networks underpinned by families, friends and frontline professionals. These networks are particularly important for vulnerable people and for anyone struck by life shocks such as bereavement or unemployment. Conservative policy should focus on empowerment of people-sized institutions that provide love, encouragement, guidance, identity and belonging.

Overleaf Guy Hordern applies this principle to the importance of fatherhood.

The importance of responsible fatherhood

Guy Hordern

Guy Hordern has been a widower since 1986. He has four children aged between 17 and 27. As well as leading courses for lone parents, Guy served as a magistrate, a school governor and a city councillor for many years. He lives in Birmingham and is Deputy Chairman of Edgbaston Constituency Conservative Association.

In January 2002, the *Guardian* published an imaginative analysis of the Government's social exclusion policies.[1] Instead of looking at various initiatives in isolation, Alison Benjamin told the story of Lean Street – a fictional community where all initiatives were in force simultaneously. What did this tell us about the Government's approach to poverty? The most obvious point was that Lean Street is a fantasy. The Social Exclusion Unit is a prolific manufacturer of Government programmes, but few of these even come close to providing universal coverage. It is as if we had an NHS that only provided cancer care to the people of Cornwall and reserved heart surgery to the citizens of Newcastle. By announcing one new programme after another, the Government can create every impression of a great social work in progress. In reality, the assorted pilot schemes, pathfinder programmes and action zones do not amount to much. This is government by press release and token gesture. The mark it makes on poverty will never be more than a scratch. But what if Lean Street were no fantasy? What if the millions or billions required to universalise each and every scheme and project were to be found? A dream come true? Or is there something dark about this fantasy?

First of all, we should be clear that there is nothing fantastic about the range of social problems experienced by the residents of Lean Street. Behind one door we are introduced to a pregnant schoolgirl, behind another a teenage delinquent and his truanting kid brother. A retired couple live in fear of crime at number 16, other residents suffer from joblessness and alcohol dependency. There are neighbourhoods like this throughout Britain, where families and communities have shattered, leaving individuals bereft of spiritual, social and material support. For every problem, the Social Exclusion Unit appears to have a solution. But not one of these involves repairing the networks of family and community in which individuals find dignity and independence. Instead, all help is to come from Whitehall direct to your door. The residents of Lean Street may live side by side, but in the eyes of the SEU each man, woman and child may as well live on an island of their own. As Oliver Letwin said, for New Labour there is no such thing as society, only the state.

Nowhere is this one-dimensional attitude to welfare more pronounced than in official approaches to family breakdown. If one were to visit a family home in Lean Street one might find something missing. There wouldn't be enough money, of course. But the house would probably be warm, adequately furnished and with food in the cupboards. In some instances one would find unacceptable material deprivation, but more often the biggest hole in a child's life would be the absence of a parent – usually their father.

Father absence

Nationwide, approximately three-quarters of fathers live with their children and the children's mother, but nearly one-quarter do not.[2] This proportion has more than doubled in less than twenty years.[3] There are 1.7 million lone parents in Britain today caring for around three million children. Nine out of ten of them are women.[4] The increase in the scale of father absence over the last two decades is associated with important shifts in its causes. In 1984 single (never married) women accounted for only one-quarter of lone mothers. In 1997 it was more than four in ten[5]. Contrary to fevered media reports about the lifestyles of the rich and famous on the one hand or the so-called 'underclass' on the other, this change has not been due to a great increase in women making a deliberate choice for lone motherhood. Indeed, over the last twenty years there has been little increase in the percentage of solely registered births.[6,7] Rather, the reason is increasing levels of relationship breakdown, especially of cohabiting relationships.

Obviously one also needs to consider the frequency with which children see non-resident fathers. Research suggests that for four in ten of these children this is at least once a week, and at least once a month for a further two in ten. This leaves four in ten who see their fathers less than once a month, including one in ten who never see their fathers at all.[8] Other research suggests that in about forty per cent of all divorces, fathers lose effective contact with their children after two years.[9] There is, therefore, no doubt that hundreds of thousands, if not millions, of children have little or no contact with their fathers.

None of this is intended as a criticism of the heroic role of lone parents, mostly lone mothers. But father absence does matter. In sixteen years of working with lone parents, I have found that the great majority did not choose to become lone parents, and would prefer to share the parenting of their children with a loving and helpful adult of the opposite sex. Moreover, because they know how hard it is to be a lone parent, they do not want their children to become lone parents themselves. And of course we must understand that father absence and lone parenthood are not one and the same issue. Many two-parent families are for various reasons 'under-fathered'. And, of course, there are children in care or living with grandparents that lack both father and mother. In short, what we need is an honest national conversation about fatherhood that goes beyond old-fashioned debates about lone parenthood. Nor should we be fixated with the issue of benefits. Of course, financial support is usually necessary where fathers are absent, but money provides care in just one dimension and cannot make up for the loss of the three-dimensional care represented by active and responsible fathers.

Fathers: unique and irreplaceable

Fathers are unique because they offer skills and instincts that are different from those provided by a mother. Fathers are irreplaceable because they offer holistic care that money, whether from the state or from a job, cannot make up for. The influence of a father is crucial to boys and girls as they grow from infancy through adolescence and into adulthood. From a child's point of view a father is important because he takes responsibility for the family, attempts to answer their questions, shows kindness and compassion, and cares for them and their mother. As they grow older it will be their father who lays down, and enforces, boundaries for them and sets an example of reliability and integrity. Their father will help them to find and face challenges in their lives and he will he there to give them time, encouragement and praise, and help them pick themselves up if and when things go wrong. Eventually he will help them leave home to launch out on their own adult lives.

That children from lone-parent families are more likely than their two-parent contemporaries to suffer from poor health, educational failure, involvement in criminal activity and other negative outcomes is supported by an enormous body of research.[10] The controversy lies in explaining how family structure is linked to the life outcomes of the children concerned. Clearly factors as diverse as the emotional trauma of divorce and the reduction in income associated with family breakdown all have a part to play. However, it is the specific phenomenon of father absence that many researchers have identified as particularly damaging to children, especially boys. Don Eberly, a senior social policy advisor in the Bush administration, has documented this research.[11] Though research into, and public awareness of, the consequences of father absence is more developed in the United States, the phenomenon has been documented by both Left[12] as well as Right[13] in Britain.

Fatherhood is also important to a mother in supporting her and providing balance to the parenting of children. Mothers and fathers need their emotional 'tanks' topped up through the care of their spouses as they give out emotionally to their children. It is not surprising that lone mothers, or those in tenuous relationships, suffer higher rates of depression than those in committed relationships.[14] Children are heavily influenced by their observations of how their parents relate to each other. Mothers and fathers, ideally expressing their commitment to each other in marriage, model an adult relationship for their children and give them confidence to embark on a similar relationship themselves. Research confirms the popular perception that depriving children of such a model negatively affects their chances of maintaining relationships in adulthood.[15]

Finally, we should not forget that fatherhood is good for men! The experience of being a father and of developing fatherhood skills makes a profound contribution to the development of male identity. This is not some 'social construction' but simply what most men want and need. The procreation and nurture of small children, the knowledge of being loved by a child and the skills and self-discipline needed to bring up children generate and develop character in men. A father receives love and trust from his children that will provide him with emotional fulfilment, self-esteem and a sense of purpose. Research shows that when men are severed from their role as husbands and fathers they earn less[16], are more prone to substance abuse[17] and have increased mortality rates.[18]

Promoting responsible fatherhood

So what can be done to reconnect Britain's absent fathers to their families? And what can be done to help men develop their fatherhood skills? Back in 1999, under the direction of the family-minded Paul Boateng, then Minister of State at the Home Office, the Government began to ask the same questions. The outcome was the establishment of Fathers Direct, a Home Office-funded charity whose brief was 'to change the whole culture which surrounds fathers, which undervalues the real passion that many have for their children. Fathers Direct will tackle the invisibility of all the good fathering which goes on.'[19]

But, however well intentioned, setting up one small charity and a website does not 'change the whole culture'. That can only happen when the message that fatherhood matters is embodied in a real way for real men and their families. This needs to start with pre-fatherhood education – school and community-based programmes to teach boys and young men about the consequences and responsibilities of becoming a father; such programmes largely have a preventative approach, seeking to dissuade young men fathering children outside of a stable and solvent relationship. The next layer of support is the resourcing of fatherhood – equipping men to fulfil their responsibilities as fathers by making available information, advice and moral support; this is especially relevant where fatherhood takes place in difficult circumstances. The third and most important tier of help should be support for the family relationships in which fatherhood is sustained – in particular, the relationship between parents, including an honest look at the effectiveness of marriage as an institution that locks fatherhood into families; and, where divorce or separation is unavoidable, efforts to maintain or re-establish the bond between father and child.

So where will this help come from and how will it be funded? The second question is the easier one to answer. Measures to prevent father absence would cost the public purse much less than measures aimed at filling a father-sized gap with money. The real problem lies in imagining the structures that could deliver the multi-layered services required to support fatherhood in all its complexity. The solution lies in looking away from Whitehall and towards local communities. The last ten years have seen a flowering of family support services provided at a local level by a wide range of statutory and voluntary organisations.[20] Clearly, these grassroots bodies have, thus far, made a stronger response to the growth of father absence programmes than has central government. It ill behoves Westminster politicians to tell the trailblazers what to do, but where they can help is to bring some coordination to the system, so that central funds can be more effectively channelled to the grassroots as priorities switch from remedial to preventative action.

America's high-profile and bipartisan National Fatherhood Initiative provides an example of how national leadership can work with local innovation. A great strength of the NFI is that it is willing to take a risk on some very innovative programmes indeed. Melanie Phillips writes of the work of the Institute for Responsible Fatherhood and Family Revitalisation, a black-led organisation based in Washington, DC.[21] Instead of waiting for teenage 'deadbeat dads' to come to them, Institute workers go and find the dads – by befriending the mothers of their children. They then work with the young men, who are often out of work, into drugs and involved with crime. There is no embarrassment about telling the men that they have a moral responsibility to their children and that they must leave behind junk food, drugs, drink and violence, but equally they are encouraged to 'forgive the past' so that can make things right in the present. The Institute provides help with jobs, healthcare, education, budgeting and marriage counselling. Savings are matched dollar for dollar. In short, the programme tears up the 'non-judgementalism' of conventional social work, but it works: 73 per cent of the dads find jobs, 87 per cent stay off drugs and almost all of them start being real fathers to their children again.

Dare we take such risks in Britain? The only certainties are that current policy is failing and that it will take a wide range of grassroots organisations to deliver the right help in the varied and intensely personal situations where fatherhood is absent.

Children and fathers after divorce

Of course, there are causes of father absence that only the government can deal with. One of the most significant is the woeful record of the British courts in maintaining contact between children and fathers following divorce. The fact that there are no official statistics on the outcome of the 110,000 access cases brought by non-resident parents every year is itself a cause for concern. But given that between 35 per cent and 50 per cent of fathers lose contact with their children after separation or divorce,[22] the fear is that there is a systemic failure of the courts to make or enforce the right decisions on access. The Government appears to share these fears. The formation of the Children and Family Court Advisory and Support Service (CAFCASS) would seem to be one response, as would the intention of the Lord Chancellor's Department to give the courts new powers to deal with parents who flout contact orders.

However, these measures do not address the real issue, which is that the family courts dispense legal process in the same way that the welfare state provides help to poor – without regard to the personal relationships on which the care of vulnerable people ultimately depends. The one-dimensional care provided by the family courts begins with the Children Act, which stipulates 'the best interests of the child' as the starting point for court decisions on access. This fails to recognise the entitlement of every child to have regular contact with both their parents. In other words, priority of consideration should be given to joint custody and facilitating a joint commitment by the mother and father to the future care of their children. This is the basis of the family court system in other countries such as Sweden and it is a fundamental first step in remedying the deficiencies of the British system. Of course, there are individual cases where shared parenting is neither possible nor desirable, for instance, where there is a history of violence, abuse, drug addiction, threat of abduction or mental illness. Depending on circumstances, complete denial of access may be required, or some form of restricted or supervised access. However, to needlessly deny a child contact with a parent should itself be regarded as a form of child abuse.

Other important reforms would flow from that understanding. Divorce or separation is often accompanied by feelings of betrayal and anger. That much is understandable. What is not is that, against such a background, the future of a child should be decided within an adversarial system of law. The courts should first encourage, and if necessary require, separating couples to attend counselling sessions. These would stress the importance of maintaining contact between the child and both parents – and then prepare each parent for a process of arbitration with the purpose of agreeing parenting arrangements with minimum recourse to lawyers and courtrooms.

However, the scope for mediation does not limit the need for reform. The relational approach to family justice is even more important where non-adversarial means fail to keep cases from the courtroom. The decisions of the court should be enforced without delay. The parent with custody (usually the mother) must not be allowed to use denial of access as a weapon against the other parent. Equally the non-resident parent (usually the father) must not be allowed to use legal procedures to bully the other parent into concessions. Clearly, the courts need new powers to guarantee enforcement, but the courts must also be able to use them effectively. This is unlikely when the hearings in an ongoing custody battle are presided over by a succession of different judges. This lack of continuity plays into the hands of parents who use delaying tactics to flout access orders – or legal technicalities to harass the other parent. In theory, continuity should be provided by the family court welfare officers, who advise the judge on each case. However, as child access cases become increasingly difficult due to complicating factors such as drug abuse, violence and the sheer mess of fractured family rela-tionships, the system is coming under strain. Speaking to frontline staff, it does not take long to establish a picture of excessive caseloads, low wages and high rates of sick leave.

All this only begins to describe the flaws in a system that struggles to dispense the law, let alone the care and attention that justice requires in family situations of such extreme sensitivity. It is clear that mere tinkering with structures, as seen in the botched formation of CAFCASS, is grossly inadequate. The entire system needs to be rebuilt around a child's need for a mum and a dad. A new 'Family Service' is required that could act with the full legal authority of the courts, but in a completely different mode focused on mediation first and then, if that fails, the effective and speedy implementation of access orders. One judge needs to take responsibility for each case from beginning to end, and judges should be assisted by properly resourced case co-ordinators who would bring in mediation specialists and other support staff as appropriate. Volunteers should also be involved, who in providing a friendly ear and unbiased advice outside of official proceedings could transform parental attitudes.

Conclusion

Of course, there would be costs in setting up such a system. But there would be savings too – both directly in terms of legal aid and court costs, and indirectly in terms of averting damage done to children deprived of their fathers. This is an analysis that should be extended to the welfare state as a whole. Can we afford to continue giving care in one dimension? Whether it is legal process or cash benefits, what the state provides cannot substitute for the three-dimensional relationships which sustain us all. What we need is not a welfare state, but a welfare society that works with the grain of humanity, not against it.

1   Alison Benjamin, 'In an ideal world', *Guardian*, 16 January 2002
2   *One parent families today – the facts*, National Council for One Parent Families,

Guy Hordern

September 2001; see also Office of National Statistics, *Social Trends*, volume 32, 2002

3   Office of National Statistics, op. cit.

4   National Council for One Parent Families, op. cit.

5   Moss, Holtermann, Owen and Brannen, 1999; reported in *Family Briefing Paper*, volume 12, Family Policy Studies Centre, February 2000

6   Office of National Statistics, *Social Trends*, volume 32, 2002

7   Moreover, sole registration does not necessarily imply that the mother would not have preferred to be in a situation where the birth could have been jointly registered.

8   McGlone, Park and Roberts, 1996, reported in *Family Briefing Paper*, volume 12, Family Policy Studies Centre, February 2000

9   *Children First*, Department of Social Security, July 1998

10 For one of the best summaries see Jill Kirby's *Broken Hearts*, Centre for Policy Studies, 2002

11 'Families, Fathers and the Making of Democratic Citizens', *Essays on Civil Society*, The Civil Society Project

12 'Boys, Young Men and Fathers: A Ministerial Seminar', Home Office, 16 November 1998; see also Norman Dennis and George Erdos, *Families without Fatherhood*, IEA Health and Welfare Unit, 1992

13 Norman Dennis and George Erdos, op. cit.

14 Kessler and Essex, 'Marital status and depression: The importance of coping resources', *Social Forces*, 1982

15 Cherlin et al, 'Parental divorce in childhood and demographic outcomes in young adulthood', *Demography*, 1995

16 Gray and Vanderhart, *The Ties that Bind: Perspectives on Marriage and Cohabitation*' Aldine de Grutyer, 2000

17 Bachman et al, *Smoking, Drinking and Drug Use in Young Adulthood*, Lawrence Erlbaum Associates, 1997

18 Hu and Goldman, 'Mortality differentials by marital status: An international comparison', *Demography*, 1990

19 Adrienne Burgess, Fathers Direct, *Observer*, 25 April 1999

20 *National Mapping of Family Services in England and Wales*, National Family and Parenting Institute, 2001

21 Melanie Phillips, *America's social revolution*, Civitas, September 2001

22 *Observer*, 21 October 2001

Six

One-size-doesn't-fit-all

The infinitely varied needs and aspirations of people cannot be met by centralised and uniform state provision. Centralised services cannot serve local diversity. Uniformity cannot respond to personal circumstances. Vulnerable people, who are most dependent on public services, are worst affected by their failure. Enterprise is not just an economic phenomenon but represents a spirit of innovation and flexibility that can bring new life and dynamism to Britain's public services. But innovation and diversity cannot flourish under the dead hand of central control. Teachers, doctors, nurses, police officers and other frontline professionals should enjoy greater freedom to serve local communities.

Overleaf Karen West applies this principle to Britain's schools.

Different schools for different children

Karen West

Specialising in secondary mathematics, Karen West was a teacher for eleven years in state and independent schools in Britain and America. She now devotes her time to looking after her two small children in Croydon.

'How can you govern a country that has 246 kinds of cheese?' asked Charles de Gaulle. Politicians despair of complexity, especially the ones that think it is their job to manage everything. The task is impossible, but somehow that doesn't stop them having a go.

Of course we all need the same laws to live by, the same taxes to pay, the same rights to enjoy. All these things are important, but they are simple – simple enough for politicians to cope with anyway. But what about the complicated things? Earning a living, raising a family, getting an education? How can the same system possibly apply to everyone? Never mind 246 kinds of cheese, what about sixty million kinds of people? One size doesn't fit all, but politicians who want to stay in charge have to pretend otherwise. It is impossible to cater for so many different needs without giving power away.

When governments do try to 'have it all' the consequences can be farcical, more often infuriating and sometimes tragic. I believe that a tragedy is unfolding in our schools. Our children are being forced through a one-size-fits-all system and it is blighting their lives and those of their parents and their teachers. Something is going desperately wrong in the classroom and the proof of that is the unprecedented level of classroom disruption.

The breakdown of discipline in schools

Until I left the profession a few years ago, I was a secondary school teacher and experienced the problem at first hand. In one school where I worked, a disruptive pupil who'd been causing trouble elsewhere was moved into my gentle-natured tutor group. Sadly this child proceeded to bully and intimidate this new group of classmates. Being outnumbered by well-behaved children, he could not afford to stand out, so he would 'persuade' other students to damage property or make them own up to things they hadn't done. Despite threats, and worse, many children did try to tell me about the incidents. I found out then that the school line was to 'keep a record of every incident and we will eventually have enough evidence to exclude him'. It took over a year. Partly there was failure of the school management to take action, but mostly it was because government bureaucracy had tied our hands. In that time, the attitude of the other children changed, they lost their enthusiasm. Trust had been betrayed.

My experience is far from unique. Classroom disruption is a common and growing problem. The effect of just a few disruptive students can be catastrophic. For senior staff it can mean that crisis management burns up valuable time resources. For teachers it can mean carefully planned lessons are ruined, and for pupils it means that the needs of the many are neglected in order to deal with the few. The former Chief Inspector of Schools, Chris Woodhead, echoes the conclusions of teaching unions when he says: 'I am certain that the strain of dealing with disruptive children is the single most signifi- cant cause of teacher stress and demoralisation.'[1] OFSTED reports that it is the main reason why so many teachers are leaving the profession.[2]

The problem isn't just the teachers who leave. Some stay, but stress still takes its toll. The effects include physical illnesses such as headaches and stomach complaints, reduced resolve in decision-making, inability to plan and complete work and the loss of morale and confidence to control classes, all of which can lead to high levels of absence from school. Teachers off work through stress can be gone for months rather than days or weeks, contributing to a £43 million bill for sick pay in Scotland alone.[3] Teacher absences have to be covered, a tall order with many schools short-staffed at the best of times. A recent National Association of Head Teachers survey found that London schools were spending between £10,000 and £100,000 a year for supply staff.[4] We can only guess at the indirect costs as staff problems affect the quality of teaching and provides more opportunities for pupil misbehaviour to surface and develop.

Furthermore, persistent low-level disruption is spilling over into violence. The ATL teaching union believes that between 1998 and 2001 there has been a five-fold increase in physical abuse by pupils.[5] Violent attacks on public service professionals aren't limited to schools. Last year 65,000 NHS staff reported being assaulted and unions report that increasing numbers of attacks are being carried out on firefighters and council workers.[6] Hospitals are resorting to extraordinary measures to protect their staff and patients. The Royal Bristol Infirmary has set up a police unit on site in a purpose-built office. There are four policemen on site who patrol the corridors. The cost of covering this and other local hospitals is £250,000 a year.[7]

Such counter-measures are necessary, but we must deal with the problem at its root. Patterns of behaviour learned in school are being carried on into adult life. Pupils learn that they don't need to exercise self-control or respect authority. If they throw tantrums, lose their temper, become violent or destroy property the lesson is that there will be no real

163

comeback. The teaching union NAS/UWT has a blacklist of 78 of the country's most violent and disruptive pupils who are currently back in the classroom, returned to school by governing bodies or independent appeals panels, usually against the wishes of the head teacher.[8] Even when such pupils are not returned, head teachers are often obliged to take excluded pupils from another school, swapping one set of problems for another. And so schools are trapped in a one-size-fits-all system where national targets restrict the freedom of teachers to act on the basis of local knowledge and with regard to the young lives placed in their care.

Schools as communities of standards

One-size-doesn't-fit-all and this is the principle that holds the key to ending the anarchy in our schools. First of all, schools need the freedom to set out the standards of behaviour expected from children, parents and staff. This needs to be based on a strong unifying ethos without which there is no community, only an institution. Britain's popular faith schools show how ethos builds into community, and community into standards. The impressive academic record of many such schools is, of course, a factor in their popularity – as is the effort to develop a strong emotional, social and moral code in young people. What is often overlooked, however, is the sense of identity, and therefore allegiance, fostered in all members of such school communities. There is no reason why this should be limited to faith schools. However, it is all but impossible to foster it in a centrally controlled state system where individual schools are reduced to branch status in a sprawling bureaucracy.

Setting out clear standards is not enough. Schools need to be able to act upon infringements of such standards. Schools need to be able to say 'no' – 'no' to poor behaviour and, where necessary, 'no' to a disruptive pupil staying in school. Without this power schools have no way of defending the integrity of their community, which is instead sacrificed to the selfishness of the few.

The Government's use of exclusion appeals panels to force the blanket acceptance of such children undermines the authority and autonomy of schools. With further damaging consequences for the school community, the only power left to teachers in such a situation is to resign or to take industrial action. The NAS/UWT reports that, in the eighteen months to May 2002, teachers in 71 schools have threatened to strike for just this reason.[9]

All schools need to become the gatekeepers of their own communities – a privilege which this Government restricts to the private sector. It is argued that the power of schools to select pupils undermines the principle of parental choice. Obviously there is a tension, but unless school communities have some choice over their membership then cohesion and distinctiveness are lost. And without these one might ask what is left for parents to choose between. There are real dangers in the attitude that state schooling can just be taken for granted. The irresponsibility of some parents and the truanting of children is the direct outcome of a take-it-or-leave-it mentality. This is not the basis for a respectful relationship between parent, pupil and school. Choice needs to go both ways.

No child left behind

All this leaves aside the question of what is to be done with excluded pupils. Again, the principle of one-size-doesn't-fit-all must be applied. First of all, from the point of view of the excluding school we must recognise that it isn't their problem. Why should they pay for the failures of a one-size-fits-all education system that they shouldn't be part of? The current Government is inching towards a diversified system for the diverse needs of pupils. But for all the talk of 'bog-standard comprehensives', New Labour's vision of schools that specialise in different areas of academic education – whether languages, sciences or arts – misses the point. It ignores the link between poor behaviour and problems with reading and writing. Children with special needs are seven times more likely to be permanently excluded than other children.[10] In their case, the National Curriculum can interfere with learning the basics and can become a straitjacket. And for all children who aren't academically minded we need to take a long cool look at a system that consists of one academic hurdle after another, from GCSE to AS-level to A-level to university. We force them over the hurdles and call them failures when they fall – as if abstract, academic achievement was the only relevant standard of excellence.

Such pupils need smaller classes, individual timetables that take into account their strengths and weaknesses and an emphasis on positive, practical projects that develop skills for life and work. Melanie Phillips, amongst others, suggests we learn from Germany's example where vocational education in schools is respected, where employers are encouraged to invest in the system and where pupils are encouraged by the prospect of guaranteed apprenticeships.[11] Such a change in the British education system would be profound, yet possible. In fact, we cannot afford to waste the potential of our practically minded young people. It is not as if the British workforce is so highly skilled that our schools need not play their part. Our country needs to value a variety of skills. It certainly has need of them.

I believe that a diverse education system that reflects different aptitudes and abilities would do much to remove the frustration that lies at the heart of so much classroom disruption. If we show our young people that there is more than one way to excel, then more of them will give it their best shot. Of course, we cannot pretend that a one-size-fits-all curriculum is the be-all and end-all of the problem. But that makes it all the more important to remove the stress caused by inappropriate learning situations, so as to identify the cases where other factors, such as emotional insecurity and poor self-esteem, are dominant.

We need to recognise that there will be a hardcore of disruptive pupils whose deep-seated problems cannot be addressed in the mainstream context – not unless we accept a lowering of personal standards in behaviour, work and achievement in our schools, and are happy for our children to receive a poorer education as they learn that the authorities cannot, or will not, do anything to change this. The one-size-fits-all mentality is doubly culpable, both for its willingness to sacrifice the needs of the many for the few, and for its failure to do much for the few anyway.

Even amongst these few we need to differentiate between the various factors, conditions and life histories by which we seek to explain their extremes of behaviour. The need for specialist care should be self-evident and until it is provided, without gaps, then we will continue as a society that doesn't deal with people, but dumps them as 'problems' on those without the power to object.

For too long we have been told that a caring society is one that treats everyone as if they were the same. But it is for the good of everyone that we must recognise that we are all different and that society should treat us as such.

1   Chris Woodhead, *Class War*, Little Brown, 2002, chapter 1

2   Damian Green, *Hansard*, column 166, 21 May 2002

3   'Warning of costs of stress in classroom', *The Times*, 8 May 2002

4   'Inquiry call as supply teacher costs soar up to 40 per cent', *Guardian*, 26 March 2002,

5   Damian Green, op. cit.

6   'Public servants get law to deter attackers', *Daily Telegraph*, 24 March 2002

7   'Police patrol hospital to ward off violence', *The Times*, 22 March 2002

8   'The Unteachables', *Daily Mail*, 28 May 2002

9   'Rate of violent pupils expelled rises for first time since 1996', *Observer*, 19 May 2002

10   Phil Willis, *Hansard*, column 177, 21 May 2002

11   Melanie Phillips, *All Must Have Prizes*, Little Brown, 1996

Seven

Character counts

Free societies depend upon the character of their citizens – their honesty, courage, compassion and sense of duty. Every new generation needs to develop the habits and traits of responsible citizenship. Families, schools, faith communities and the media can contribute to, or undermine, healthy character formation. There is no neutral ground in the formation of character.

Overleaf Cameron Watt applies this principle to character education in schools.

Educating for life,
not just work

Cameron Watt

Cameron Watt is a policy analyst with the social affairs think tank Renewing One Nation. He previously taught in a comprehensive school in Hampshire, having trained as a teacher at the University of Strathclyde in Glasgow. A volunteer sports coach at his former school, Cameron has been involved in a variety of youth initiatives.

Recently I learned that one of my former pupils, a boy of fifteen preparing to sit his GCSEs, had taken his own life. This provoked the obvious question in my mind: is there anything that the school (including me) could have done that would have prevented this tragedy? On balance, I suspect not: the boy had been drinking excessively and this was probably a decisive factor in the tragedy.

Rates of suicide and self-harm amongst teenagers are alarmingly high. Indeed young people growing up in Britain today are succumbing in increasing numbers to a range of destructive behaviours including binge-drinking, experimenting with drugs, early sex and gang culture.[1] This malaise is emerging within a more coarse, nihilistic popular culture, which revels in brutality and celebrates sexual violence. Even leading liberals recognise the problem.[2] In such a culture, parents can lack the knowledge and confidence to equip their children to successfully negotiate these challenges. Many therefore hope that children will be suitably equipped with relevant information and life skills at school, or, at the very least, they expect schools to do their children no harm.

Labour are making things worse

Unfortunately, such confidence is often ill-founded. Efforts to help young people negotiate life's challenges are usually conducted in assemblies or Personal, Social and Health Education. PSHE is usually taught by non-specialists, often the pupil's form tutor. PSHE is, unsurprisingly, not a priority for most schools; although part of the National Curriculum, it is never examined. Of course that does not mean that it is not significant. This essay contends that schools' efforts to equip young people to lead fulfilled, healthy lives are often inadequate and that government-favoured approaches may actually be exacerbating some of the most acute problems facing the emerging generation. Conservative policy in these areas during our eighteen years of government was, in large measure, a failure. It is tragic that the present administration has learnt nothing from our mistakes.

Labour claim to be supporting parents but they are failing.

Muddled and contradictory social policy is compounded by the damage of Labour's attachment to ideologically hidebound organisations such as DrugScope and Brook that are driving policy and programmes in schools. These undermine parental values in condoning and excusing dangerous behaviours. Harm reduction is their guiding approach. This thinking was initially developed in the context of helping heroin addicts inject more safely. However, its logic – that people are inevitably going to engage in destructive activities and the best that can be done is to help them to do so more safely – is now regularly applied to children. Activities such as experimenting with drugs or having early sex are, of course, illegal and most parents would be opposed to them being condoned at school.

What is character education?

The future of our young people can be bright. More should be growing up able to sustain relationships and lead happy, healthy and productive lives. In spite of vast pressures to the contrary, most young people are managing to make positive choices. This needs to be constantly acknowledged, but it must not be taken for granted.

Plato argued that people do not naturally make right choices. In order for civilisation to survive, therefore, Plato contended that children must be trained to feel pleasure, liking, disgust and hatred for those things that really are pleasant, likeable, disgusting and hateful. 'Character education' is a name that can be given to the contribution that schools might make to this 'civilising' process.

Building character entails much more than equipping young

people to avoid destructive life choices, although that is obviously an essential part of it. The wider mission must be to equip young people with the attitudes, values and skills to enable them to make constructive life choices and fulfil their potential. This vision has been lost by a Labour Government that now sees education as little more than the acquisition of skills for paid work. Ann Holt describes the problem well:

> Education has always had a choice as to whether it reflects the society in which it carries out its functions or seeks in some way to shape it. Sadly, our education system too often seems to mirror our community-poor world with its emphasis on the individual, and his or her personal ambition and achievement. Schools these days feel more like factories than communities . . . there has been a tendency of late for education to puff up the 'engineering' of learning to an importance that it does not deserve . . . [There is an] emphasis on skills and information that lead to economic productivity rather than personal development.[3]

The learning of individual subjects in schools must be placed within a broader context which values and affirms every pupil. Sense of worth must not just be derived from academic or sporting achievement. Teachers and pupils must not feel so harassed by the relentless demands for 'results' that the human dimension is squeezed out. Faith schools are often good at striving for and affirming success, whilst not seeing it as an end in itself. They tend to inculcate pupils with a sense of duty and awareness of right and wrong. Can lessons be learned from faith schools that can be applied to the whole education system?

In the coming months the Renewing One Nation unit at Conservative Central Office will be exploring how teachers, schools and local groups can better help young people thrive. Initially this will entail consideration of how civil society groups can better help young people, but if we are to successfully build character in young people, serious study must be done on how existing structures and practices are undermining this goal. It seems likely that schools would be keen to try different approaches that encourage young people to avoid rather than reduce harm. However, Conservatives should not attempt to impose these from the top down – we need to give parents and schools more freedom to pursue them themselves.

Role for civil society

Civil society groups will be of growing importance in ensuring that children receive a well-rounded education. Teachers are under greater pressure than ever before, and are less likely to run extra-curricular activities. In primary and increasingly in secondary education, male teachers are becoming rare.[4] The consequent lack of positive male role models has serious implications, particularly for children from lone parent families, the vast majority of which are headed by women. Idleness (one of Beveridge's five giants) and isolation are perhaps less obvious but nonetheless acute problems for many young people. (Power companies now plan for a surge in demand during the summer as children while away the hours on their PlayStations.)[5] Provision of competitive sport can be an excellent means of overcoming these problems and keeping teenage boys engaged in secondary school. It is a vital crucible for learning values that are neglected elsewhere. (By participating in games, pupils increasingly learn the value of co-operation, hard work, self-sacrifice, deferred gratification and how to cope with setbacks, not just in sport but throughout life.) Therefore the strengthening of competitive team sport is vital for creating more healthy, well-balanced people. Civil society can make a significant contribution in this area, from the professional basketball teams who provide regular coaching in Hackney schools to the parents who can offer the occasional Saturday morning.

There are numerous other areas in which voluntary and faith-based groups can make a fuller contribution in our schools. Whilst training as a teacher, I worked at a secondary school in one of the most deprived parts of Glasgow, in the shadow of Celtic Park. Local volunteers, mainly retired people, would come in to school once a week to spend an hour listening to the reading of an academically struggling pupil in their first or second year. It was inspiring to witness the difference this made to the confidence of the pupils involved. Sport, debt education, sex and drugs lessons, community-service opportunities: all these activities and more can be better provided in school if the Government has the political will to allow better use of the people with first-hand knowledge and experience in these areas. Many do, and many more would, willingly give of their time.

Character education must pervade the whole school to be successful. It is, in essence, a positive vision for how schools can help children. However, before such a vision can be implemented, it is vital to recognise the specific ways in which young people are being failed at present. Drugs and sex education are two obvious examples of inadequate current provision. Each will be examined in turn.

Drugs education

Understandably, one of parents' greatest fears is that their children will get caught up in the drug culture. In May 2002, the Department for Education and Skills launched a new 'tougher' drugs strategy. Apparently education minister Ivan Lewis MP has insisted on a stronger moral message in schools' drugs education.[6] Central to the new approach is *Rachel's Story*, a video telling the story of Rachel Whitear. This 21-year-old's tragic solitary death after a heroin overdose was harrowingly illustrated in the media after her parents decided that it might discourage teenagers from experimenting with drugs. The Government has also promised longer sentences for those dealing drugs around school gates and automatic expulsion for children dealing in school.

Yet Labour's muddled and contradictory drugs policy highlights how they have failed to protect young people. It certainly fails to exhibit that most prized New Labour asset, 'joined-up government'. Cannabis is the illegal drug teenagers are most likely to use. Advocates of decriminalisation suggest it is less harmful than alcohol. However, any drugs worker will tell you that a teenager who starts smoking cannabis two or three times a week is likely to soon suffer a significant decline in their academic performance as their mind is clouded and their motivation wanes. Mounting evidence suggests that many young people wrongly inferred from the Lambeth experiment that the drug had been decriminalised. Their perception that the drug is harmless will almost certainly be reinforced by the powerfully symbolic decision of David Blunkett to reclassify the drug from Class B to C. Indeed after the announcement, pictures have been published in a number of papers of young adults 'skinning up' whilst soaking up the sun in London parks. Some have shown groups of young teenagers approaching the cannabis smokers and asking to join in.[7] Such sights are likely to become common.

Government has sent a clear message to young people that the consequences of taking cannabis are not that severe. Yet at the very time Government is sending out this message, increasing numbers of young people are being offered 'skunk' and other highly enriched, potent forms of cannabis that have much stronger adverse consequences than those previously available. Announced changes in policing and the law will, almost certainly, increase the availability of drugs. Yet recent research by Paul McArdle at Newcastle University has proved that high availability of drugs through peer groups can overwhelm the protective factors that help prevent drug use, such as children living with both parents.[8] Estelle Morris's DfES may have wished to promote a more 'moral' drugs policy in schools, but this has been completely undermined by the Home Office's indifference towards cannabis.

DrugScope, the self-styled 'UK's leading centre of expertise on drugs', receive substantial government funding[9] and have great influence on the formation of drugs policy and drug education in schools. They are at the forefront of campaigning for more liberal drugs laws. DrugScope espouse the virtues of what they describe as a more 'factual' approach to drugs education. However many 'factual' programmes of drugs education work on the basis that a significant proportion of young people will be using at least the 'softer' drugs and that they should be given information on how to use them more safely. Thus 'factual' approaches are effectively harm reduction approaches.

Why is this a problem? Facts are certainly vital, but they are not the sum total of education. A normative, moral element is essential in responsible drugs education. Society must have the collective nerve and sense to recognise that illegal drugs are deeply damaging. Young people should be given facts on illegal drugs, but they must also be asked to consider the destructive effects these drugs may have, not just in their own lives, but also on their families, communities and wider society. On that basis they should be encouraged to avoid drugs. Libertarian drug educators may consider themselves to have succeeded if a young person takes drugs, so long as they are aware of the 'facts'. For libertarians, taking drugs is not about what is good or bad, right or wrong for society; it is about individuals autonomously authenticating themselves through so called personal 'lifestyle' choices.

Good 'harm avoidance' approaches never use preachy or simplistic 'just say no' messages. For example DARE – Drug

Abuse Resistance Education – deliver a life skills programme, providing young people with the assertiveness to make positive decisions, having considered the likely consequences – good and bad – of choices they face. DARE also produce a detailed Drug Awareness Handbook, sponsored by local businesses, giving parents the information they need. However these community-based harm avoidance initiatives, though popular and successful, do not fully concur with the fashionable consensus on drugs education and therefore receive little or no funding from statutory bodies. The DARE approach also understands that risk behaviours are closely connected. The skills taught by DARE will help young people to avoid other potentially self-destructive choices. The lack of coherence in Government departments' approach to drug policy has already been discussed. There is a much deeper confusion as to how approaches to drugs, sex, tobacco and alcohol, for example, relate to each other. Policymakers and educators need to understand that involvement in one risk behaviour often leads to exposure to others and a tough approach to one risk behaviour will be undermined by a weak approach to another.

Sex education and sexual health

The current approach to sex education and reducing teenage pregnancies exemplifies Labour's failed 'one-size-fits-all' approach to helping young people avoid destructive choices. Over the last thirty years, contraceptive-rich but values-deficient sex education has been promoted.[10] This has coincided with great pressure to extend 'family planning' and 'sexual health' services to young people, including those under the age of consent. The latest stage in this trend is the Government's decision in July 2002 to extend clinics in schools that will hand out contraceptives to children as young as eleven.

Britain has the highest rate of teenage pregnancies in Western Europe.[11] There are 90,000 teenage conceptions a year; 7,700 to under-sixteens.[12] The proportion of teenage conceptions outside of marriage has risen from forty per cent in 1978 to ninety per cent currently.[13] There has been a sharp rise in the levels of new cases of sexually transmitted infections (STIs) since 1995 and teenagers have suffered the biggest increases in rates of infection. For example, there was a 74 per cent increase in cases of gonorrhoea in girls under sixteen between 1995 and 2000, and a 107 per cent rise in diagnoses of chlamydia in under-age girls over the same period.[14] Perhaps surprisingly, the number of young women attending family planning clinics has risen considerably – between 1989 and 1999, the number of attendances by girls under the age of sixteen rose from 18,000 to 68,000, while attendances by women overall remained the same.[15]

Recent research by Dr David Paton of Nottingham University has found no evidence that providing family planning reduces either underage conception or abortion rates among under-sixteens in Britain. He says:

> Over the past few years, we have had a massive expansion in family planning services for young people in the UK . . . Although family planning may make sexually active teenagers less likely to get pregnant, it seems that it also encourages others to start having sex.

Some of these will get pregnant through contraceptive failure and, if anything, the overall effect of expanding family planning services for under-sixteens has been to increase pregnancies and abortions.[16]

Commenting on this, Labour MP Jim Dobbin bravely warned his increasingly ideologically blinkered party:

This is not about the morality of abortion. It is not about the morality of distributing contraception to the very young. It is about the morality of adopting strategies when there is no clear indication as to their potential success and a considerable amount of evidence as to the damage they do.[17]

When confronted by the abject failure of sex education to improve outcomes for young people, the sex education industry wriggle around. They offer a string of excuses or blame teachers for not being well enough trained. They suggest sex education is not given enough time in the curriculum. In short, they prescribe more of the same. However there is clear evidence that even the 'new, improved' programmes are failing to deliver. For example, an extensive study, published in the *British Medical Journal*, on the twenty-session Safe, Happy and Responsible (SHARE) programme operating in Scottish schools, showed that it failed in its stated aims to reduce unwanted pregnancies and unsafe sexual behaviour.[18] Undeterred, the Scottish Health Education Board is planning to extend the programme across the country.

There is such a thing as society

A major problem with the term 'young people' is that it is commonly used to refer to those aged twenty as well as twelve. In literature produced by the sex education industry, there is often a blurring of the lines between who is an adult and a child, between what is legal and illegal. In some instances, this appears to be deliberate. For example Brook, who receive substantial statutory funding, offer the following legal advice to under sixteens on their website:

> Although, strictly speaking, it's illegal for someone to have sex with a girl under 16, we know that maturity does not suddenly arrive on the 16th birthday, and that many young people are mature enough to make their own decisions about their lives.[19]

Distinctions between legal and illegal activity may be considered unhelpful to those for whom the right of the very young to sexual experimentation is an article of faith. But if the state and its agencies ignore law designed to protect children, what is the point in having that law? Even if very difficult to enforce, surely the purpose of an age of consent is in the message it sends to society: children are harmed by having sex and the state will do what it can to protect them from such harm. Labour is sending out the very opposite message. In addition, the current approach with its chemical 'quick fixes' suggests that actions need not have consequences. It is also implies that there is a drug to deal with every eventuality. This is the soma of Huxley's Brave New

World. 'Sexual health' provision may encourage experimentation, but there are still no cures for serious sexual infections such as HIV and hepatitis B, let alone the emotional pain and damage to future relationships that early sex can cause.

Commenting on the decision to extend 'Bodyzone' clinics to schools around the country, Iain Duncan Smith said:

> Giving contraception in schools is a wrong move by the Government because it undermines parental authority. Decisions are being detached from schools and parents and given to central authorities. These people do not have to pick up the pieces if this policy goes wrong.[20]

Government policy is seriously undermining parents' right to be fully involved in every aspect of their children's upbringing. If the Scottish experience tells us anything, it demonstrates that the overwhelming majority of parents in England and Wales would be against the repeal of Section 28 (the legislation preventing local authorities spending money on the promotion of homosexuality in schools or elsewhere). However the irresponsibility of some agencies involved in PSHE in schools clearly indicates that a widening of the legislation is needed. NHS health trusts, under the pretext of healthy living, have been distributing harmful, and unnecessarily explicit, heterosexual and homosexual material in schools.[21] 'Health promotion' is not covered by Section 28 and therefore offers an easy means of subverting the legislation. This

185

loophole should be closed by extending the existing legislation to cover harmful material relating to all sexual orientations. Extension of Section 28 would both end the unnecessary offence caused by the possible implication that the only pernicious propaganda targeted on schoolchildren is of a homosexual nature and it would provide children with better protection. Conservatives should promote programmes of sex education that emphasise the skills that are necessary to sustain relationships and ultimately marriage. In spite of the efforts of David Blunkett during his time as Education Secretary, Labour has clearly not achieved this.

Schools of Character

As one American author and former Education Secretary, William Bennett, has put it:

> Schools are helping to cultivate moral sensibilities, to shape character, every day. Students notice whether teachers go about their work conscientiously or lazily, enthusiastically or begrudgingly. They see how adults in the school address one another, the students, and their parents. They see with what care (or lack thereof) the school building and ground are maintained. And they learn, too, from the assignments they are given and the evaluations they receive. In all these ways, habits of feeling, thought, and action are being cultivated: Character is being formed.[22]

Cameron Watt

New Labour's statist social engineering has betrayed the emerging generation. It's time for a new approach. Teachers want to be more than mere conduits of centrally devised curricula. Those entering the profession are, to a greater or lesser extent, idealistic. They want to play a positive part in shaping the next generation. They want to build character.

Government must harness the idealism and professionalism of teachers to this end. Head teachers, boards of governors and classroom practitioners must be entrusted with the task of delivering the education parents want. They must have the freedom to decide whether to try approaches aimed at enabling their pupils to avoid, rather than merely reduce, harm from the challenges they face. All schools should have the freedom to determine their own ethos and values, free from the meddling of the local education authority or central government. The social policy elite, in large part contemptuous of the values and aspirations of mainstream voters, will be understandably opposed to this, but we are not. Conservatives trust the people.

---

1   There has been a steep rise in under-age drinking since 1990, especially among boys, but there are now signs of a levelling off. The amount drunk by 11–15 year old drinkers doubled from 1990 to 1998 (E. Goddard and V. Higgins, *Smoking, Drinking and Drug Use among Young Teenagers in 1998*, volume 1, Office of National Statistics, 1999). The prevalence of drug use among 12–13 year olds has increased fivefold, and among 14–15 year olds eightfold, since 1987 (Standing Conference on Drug Abuse / Children's Legal Centre, *Young People and Drugs*, 1999). There has been a sharp rise in the levels of new cases of sexually transmitted infections since 1995 and teenagers have suffered the biggest increases in rates of infection. For example, there was a 74

per cent increase in cases of gonorrhoea in girls under sixteen between 1995 and 2000, and a 107 per cent rise in diagnoses of chlamydia in under-age girls over the same period (Public Health Laboratory Service, *Trends in sexually transmitted infections in the United Kingdom 1990–1999*)

2   See, for example Jonathan Freedland, 'Nation in Bondage', *Guardian*, 17 July 2002

3   Ann Holt, 'Communities or Factories?', R Briefing, The Relationships Foundation, November 2001

4   The proportion of male recruits to secondary teacher training has slumped from 43 per cent to 36 per cent over five years. Only thirteen per cent of the recruits to primary teacher training are men (Rebecca Smithers, 'Teacher colleges recruit fewer men', *Guardian*, 15 July 2002.

5   'Children suffering "September-itis"', BBC News Online, 2 September 2001

6   'Government tackles drugs education in schools', Department for Education and Skills press release, 21 May 2002

7   *Daily Mail*, 15 July 2002

8   Paul McArdle et al., 'European adolescent substance use: the roles of family structure, function and gender', *Addiction*, volume 97, May 2002, pages 329–336

9   For example, for the year 2002/03, jointly with the Department of Health, the Drug Education and Prevention Team at DrugScope have been given a grant of £106,300 'to promote good practice' in the delivery of Personal, Social and Health Education in schools. DrugScope now have an annual income of over £4 million, the substantial majority of which comes from government sources (David Miliband, *Hansard*, column 990W, 10 July 2002).

10   The Education Reform Act 1988 placed the responsibility for sex education in the hands of school governors. All schools must have a policy on Sex and Relationships Education (SRE). The July 2000 SRE guidance from the Department for Education and Skills states that schools should work with parents and others in the local community in delivering SRE. In practice governors have a very limited range of outside agencies to work with. At present organisations with the significant resources needed to work in schools are mostly local family planning clinics and national bodies such as Brook and FPA which are in receipt of substantial government money. Groups offering alternatives to the failed Brook type approaches receive little or no statutory funding, making it difficult for them to work with schools which would value their services.

11   Social Exclusion Unit, *Teenage Pregnancy*, 1999

12   Ibid.

13   Ibid.

14   Public Health Laboratory Service, *Trends in sexually transmitted infections in the United Kingdom 1990–1999*

15   Department of Health, *NHS Contraceptive Services, England: 1999–2000*, 2000

16   D Paton, 'The economics of family planning and underage conceptions', *Journal of Health Economics*, volume 21, 2002, pages 207–225.

17   ''Benny Hill culture' blamed for teenage pregnancies', *Daily Telegraph*, 18 July 2002

18   Daniel Wight et al., 'Limits of teacher delivered sex education: interim behavioural outcomes from randomised trial', *British Medical Journal*, 15 June 2002

19   www.brook.org.uk/under16.htm, July 2002

20   'School clinics to give pupils free condoms', *Daily Telegraph*, 28 June 2002

21   An example of such harmful material isYoung People's Guide, Birmingham Health Authority/Birmingham Leisure and Community Services, 1998.

22   William J Bennett and Edwin J Delattre, 'Character, the Old-Fashioned Way', *Weekly Standard*, 20 August 2001

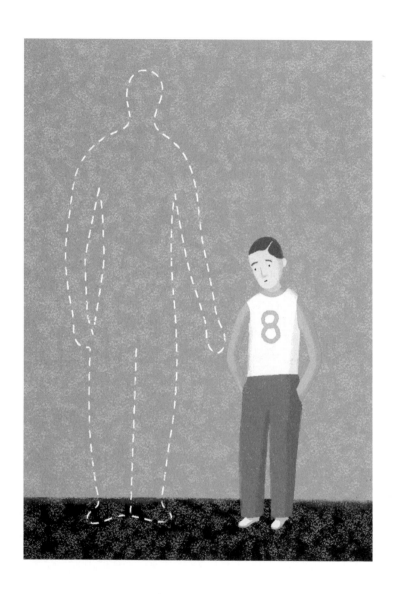

Eight

A good society needs good neighbours

A much greater sense of duty throughout society is necessary for the renewal of the nation's social capital. Western societies may have conquered economic and technological frontiers but they have failed to provide many very vulnerable people with the most basic forms of companionship. Only very strong people can overcome adversity alone. More must be done to prevent life shocks from becoming major life crises for affected people. A citizen's responsibilities not only include the payment of taxes but also a willingness to befriend and support neighbours in need.

Overleaf Dan Munford and Nadine Dorries apply this principle to youth offending.

Rebuilding the neighbourly society

Dan Munford and Nadine Dorries

Dan Munford is a former Liberal Democrat parliamentary candidate and researcher who recently joined the Conservative Party, which he sees as the most innovative and open forum for the development of social policy. Dan works as a senior partner with the market research company Insight Research. He lives in Powys with his wife and their two children.

Nadine Dorries was born in Liverpool and originally trained as a nurse. Since then she has run her own businesses as well as a community school in central Africa, before going on to serve as a director of a major healthcare company. She was the Conservative candidate in Hazel Grove at the last election and is now an adviser on youth offending policy to the Shadow Home Secretary Oliver Letwin MP. Nadine is married and the mother of three daughters.

Despite increasing standards of living, crime is on the rise again. British people are statistically far more likely to become victims of crime than are citizens in other developed countries, 54.5 crimes per 100 inhabitants compared with an average of 35.2 per 100.[1] Certain crimes, particularly those likely to involve young people, have exploded in the last year.[2] Street robberies increased dramatically in 2001 and the majority of offenders were youths.[3] Young people account for approximately one-third of all criminal offences in the UK.[4] Most young offenders start to commit crime at age fifteen, one year after they begin to absent themselves from both school and home.[5]

In 1997 a new Labour Government came to office convinced that it understood the root causes of crime for young offenders. Numerous initiatives seemed to indicate an understanding of the problem. The Youth Justice Board and subsequently the Youth Offending Teams were exciting initiatives. The emphasis on restorative justice, reparation and the establishment of referral panels seemed impressive. Unfortunately, despite the fact that the Government has thrown 'everything' at youth crime, such initiatives appear to have made very little difference.

Government has increasingly used the language of social science. Experts can identify the so called 'risk factors' that indicate a pre-school child is likely to mature to commit crime in their adolescent and adult years. Unfortunately, as Shadow Home Secretary Oliver Letwin has contended, although the present system has increased the state's ability to recognise likely future offenders it still fails at every level to lead the 'problem child' away from the 'conveyor belt of crime' from the age of four or five onwards.[6]

Many of the children who become persistent young offenders grow up in dysfunctional homes. Children who grow up uncared for are likely to show behavioural problems by the age of five.[7] Although many of them have 'parents' this does not mean that they are 'parented'. From a very early age they often live in indescribable circumstances, surviving alone by their own wits and ability. The absence of love and constancy nurtures emotionally void and dangerous human beings who lack capacity to experience empathy or remorse.

At school these children become an inconvenience and a problem that so far evades the system's ability to categorise. Unless they are seen to be physically at risk Social Service 'Care' (itself a failing system) does not intervene. They start a life of petty crime and move on to serious crime. They serve their first prison sentence, come out and repeat the offence. They are then given a longer prison sentence.

Very many young people in care become young people in prison. Figures from the National Prison Survey suggest that 38 per cent of prisoners under the age of 21 have been in local authority care.[8] The Youth Justice System also fails in its rehabilitative role. Re-offending rates in Young Offenders Institutions are roughly 75 per cent.[9] The system only protects the public against young offenders for the duration of their sentence.

In perpetuating this system, the state is not tackling the roots of crime. It is judging children – in identifying them as future liabilities – without helping them. As a consequence it is failing to reduce the risk to society and, more fundamentally, is depriving children of their opportunity of redemption. By contrast Conservatives believe that human beings, though imperfect, all have the capacity to find redemption, to change and to fulfil their own individual promise.

The collapse of social capital

New ideas from the United States may assist our search for solutions. Robert Putnam's influential work – *Bowling Alone – the Collapse and Revival of American Community* – has become central to much political discussion in America and Britain.[10] Putnam's analysis of the underlying causes of the collapse and revival of civic association in America may also provide us with a better understanding of the nature of our own problems.

Putnam shows how – over the last 25 years – Americans have become disconnected from friends, family, neighbours and social structures, from bowling leagues, political parties, sports clubs, churches or parent-teacher associations. The consequent reduction in 'social capital', the loss of trust in the community, organisational participation and social cohesion, represents a serious threat to the civic health.

The decline of social capital affects all neighbourhoods and parts of the UK. But it is most significant in its impact upon the lives of people in hardest-pressed inner-city areas. Affluence and education offer no immunity against collective tragedy but for particularly vulnerable groups – like children in poorer areas –

social capital is of disproportionate importance. Children, above all, need social capital to 'grow up right'. Its absence can lead to a neighbourhood rapidly spiralling out of control, as we are starting to see in parts of London. Recent figures showed that half of all UK robberies could be traced back to only twenty local council areas, headed by Lambeth in south London.[11]

In low-income neighbourhoods, informal social control amongst residents – based upon mutual trust and altruism among neighbours or the willingness to interfere if they see children misbehaving – are more important than membership of formal programmes.[12] As good neighbours and role models disappear or decline in influence, and as unemployment and poverty become more widespread, children become vulnerable to a variety of social ills.[13]

Putnam finds that 'the absence of positive norms, community associations, and informal adult friendship and kin networks leaves kids to their own devices' and it is in such a setting that the neighbourhood gangs flourish and 'bad things happen to good kids'. In this environment a small number of hardened young criminals can come to dominate the streets. Sir John Stevens, Commissioner of the Metropolitan Police, believes that that there are typically twenty seasoned young criminals in any one London borough.[14]

In the last forty years we have experienced increasing disengagement from civic life. Much of society has been transformed from one based upon place-based connections to one based upon non-place-based relationships. Many have thrived and adapted to new possibilities. But in times of rapid social change, some people adapt more quickly than others. Vulnerable people have often found themselves left behind and disproportionately disadvantaged as reserves of social capital – the formal and informal networks of birth and location rather than of choice – have become increasingly depleted.

Putnam's analysis of US society has obvious parallels with the UK. Putnam details the time we spend on solitary commutes from our suburban sprawl, shopping in one place, living in another, and working in a third. This kind of existence fails to satisfy one of Dr Michael Schluter's five key indicators of healthy relationships. Healthy relationships require regularity and consistency of contact but this is lacking for many people today. In particular, contends Schluter, relationships can be weak and unsustainable if they lack face-to-face contact; are infrequent or irregular; are not sustained in more than one role or context; are unequal because of basis in role or status; and, are not built on common ends or experience.[15] Relationships may also be less healthy and sustainable today, because without the context of strong extended family and other support networks, people do not have the reserves to call upon when difficulties strike.

Robert Putnam forces us to consider the impact technology and the mass media have upon how we spend our leisure time. Television has profoundly affected our lives. The average Briton now watches roughly 3.7 hours per day.[16] US husbands and wives spend three or four times as much time watching television together as talking to each other, and six to seven times as much as they spend in community activities outside the home. More television watching means less of virtually every other (face-to-face) form of civic participation.[17]

Changing patterns of work also have had a significant impact. Women, historically 'the neighbourhood builders', are now much more likely to be away at work during daytime than their mothers were. Professional men, the bedrock of neighbourhood associations, are also spending longer hours working than their fathers did.

In the early nineteenth century Alexis de Tocqueville had been impressed by Americans' passion for civic association but the later part of the century was an intense period of change with rapid urbanisation, immigration and industrialisation. Americans became strangers to each other. But subsequently social capital was recovered during the 'progressive era' and Putnam believes that this natural process of renewal should happen again.

During the period of intense social dislocation, the US experienced crime waves, urban degradation, inadequate education, a widening gap between rich and poor and political corruption. But according to Putnam: 'Even as these problems were erupting, America was beginning to fix them. A sense of crisis, coupled with inspired grass roots and national leadership produced an extraordinary burst of inventiveness and political reform.' This collective effort saw many of the major community institutions in American life invented or restored – the YMCA, Red Cross, Boy Scouts and the National League of Cities.

Britain had itself met a similar challenge earlier in the nineteenth century. The municipality movement was a response to problems arising from the rapid and unplanned growth of huge industrial cities. It created new civic institutions in city schools, housing, libraries and public drainage schemes, recreating its social capital stock and finding new leaders like Lord Shaftesbury and Thomas Barnardo. This period in British history witnessed the formation of the Scouts as well as the Sunday school movement. In the early stages of British industrialisation Professor Christie Davies contends that church, friendly societies and other Victorian institutions compensated for the loosening of family and village bonds. Friendly societies were based on encounter relationships that minimised false claims and the relationships were close enough for effective policing of deserving and undeserving cases. Davies writes: 'Whereas in Britain in the last half of the nineteenth century people responded to urban anonymity and uncertainty by the spontaneous creation of institutions that provided new personal relationships and a stronger personal moral ethic, in the twentieth century all British institutions and moral thinking have become permeated with an impersonal ethos.'[18]

Rebuilding social capital

In rebuilding social capital today, our first step must be to recognise the character of the problem. The breakdown of the ultimate form of social capital – the nuclear family – over the last forty years has not gone unnoticed by researchers, social commentators and politicians. The quality of a child's parenting is the most important ingredient in their long-term development and many of the children who later become young offenders grow up in dysfunctional homes. Yet one child in every four in the UK has only one parent looking after them.[19] The UK's rate of teenage pregnancy is the highest in Europe.[20]

By contrast stable families can have a substantial effect upon the communities they live in or move out of. Putnam found that the presence of many stable families in a community is associated with lower levels of youthful law-breaking because they tend to produce well-adjusted children. 'Good' families can produce a ripple affect by increasing the pool of 'good peers' that other families can befriend. If youth trouble-making is a form of communicable disease – 'a sort of behavioural chicken pox' that spreads through high schools and friendship groups – then stable families provide the vaccines that reduce the number of contagious children capable of 'infecting others'.

The state could act more compassionately to help families, as other essays in this book illustrate. But although the state can identify the problem in families, it can only be part of the solution. Putnam's research on the solutions invented in nine-teenth- and early twentieth-century America also shows that individuals and organisations can be expected to emerge to bring hope with inspirational grassroots leadership. This natural process requires more encouragement from the state and a willingness to knock down the artificial walls that exist between public services and civil society. Getting voluntary and community groups more involved with schools, hospitals and social services would not simply make sense in terms of public sector reform, it would also help build up social capital in the places where vulnerable children and their families live.

Grassroots leadership typically features individuals or organisations with a strong social entrepreneurial commitment to right wrongs. At its best, this kind of community leadership can be far more adaptable than can the state.

Camilla Batmanghelidjh is one individual who has not waited for the state to own up to its failure. Through her work with excluded children, Camilla came to appreciate the inability of the existing system to deal with the problem. Like Thomas Barnardo in the nineteenth century, she has reached the conclusion that certain children desperately need substitute parents to save their lives from crisis.

She identified a large group of children who had never been nurtured; were not fed, clothed or cared for; many of whom were living in homes with no gas, electricity, or food; and with no adult contact or supervision for much of the week. These children were often at 'the end of the road' with nowhere to go and no one to go to. The authorities had given up on them. They were unable to access care via normal routes and those which Camilla saw in schools were on the verge of expulsion. Staff turnover, pupil violence and sheer workload mean that no action is taken. Teachers may notice and worry when a child struggles with the acceptance of some of the most basic social norms but as long as the problem is moral and physical the system has no resources to help.

Camilla realised that these children needed extra support and this realisation inspired her to establish 'The Place to Be'. This programme involved placing psychologists in schools who could work with children as required: when a dispute broke out children could be taken straight into counselling, for example. Rather than asking parents to take children to counselling (which never happened), counsellors were on site. The aim was to give children someone to go to so that they could 'offload' their problems and seek assistance before a dangerous threshold was passed.

Batmanghelidjh's Kids Company takes this one stage further by catering for socially excluded children who pass their daytimes on the street.[21] It offers unparented children a place of safety, care and learning in the community that will help normalise their social development. Up to 200 children pass through the centre every day. No child is turned away. Ages range from three to twenty.

Children who arrive are clothed and given hot meals. There are people to talk to who want to listen. Hugs and cuddles are given when appropriate. Children are health checked and registered with a dentist and a GP. Teachers provide education for children who have been excluded from school. There is a library and drama and recording studios. Qualified staff help with housing and benefit claims, the youth justice system, and with health and other problems. Standards of cleanliness are exceptional. Graffiti or litter is not allowed. Good behaviour is rewarded with points that can be used for 'shopping'.

Hallmarks of good neighbour projects

Projects like Kids Company often succeed where conventional, bureaucratised approaches fail because of a range of inherent advantages:

- Firstly, they possess first-hand local knowledge and at their best they function 24 hours a day, seven days a week.
- Secondly, they offer personal care. One-size-doesn't-fit-all and community-based projects are flexible enough to respect the unique circumstances of the person in need. This flexibility owes much to their ability to mobilise volunteers who can care for people on a one-to-one basis.
- Thirdly, community-based projects tend to be values-based. Faith-based groups, for example, apply the teachings of their faith to the circumstances of those they seek to help.
- Fourthly, good neighbour projects are often led by people with real experience of the problems at hand. Prisoner support ministries are run by reformed ex-prisoners. Men who have conquered addictions work with people currently struggling with drugs. Streetwise grandmothers mentor abandoned single mums.

It is essential that public policy is reinvented to resource and support these good neighbour projects. Essential to such a reinvention will be a more mature attitude to risk. Public policy-makers need to be willing to take well-judged risks by permitting – perhaps indirectly – investment in innovative community-based projects that will care for the vulnerable people who are being reliably failed by existing schemes. Bad news stories invariably receive more press attention than good news and politicians fear association with projects that might fail in headline-grabbing ways. This means that established approaches win funding much more often than they should. Social reformers like Barnardo and Shaftesbury were sometimes seen as dangerous radicals in their own time. They succeeded in overcoming their doubters. One might ask whether they would have been allowed to develop their ideas in twenty-first-century Britain. It is telling that Kids Company has already run into various difficulties with the authorities.[22]

Conclusion

Although today's young people did not initiate the erosion of the UK's social capital, their parents did and it remains the obligation of British citizens to help re-establish civic engagement amongst new generations. Individually we all have a responsibility to rebuild social capital. In government we have a responsibility to encourage those who do so.

1   According to the International Crime Victim Survey of 2000, crime per head in England and Wales was higher than any of the seventeen other countries in the survey.

2   Home Office recorded crime figures, July 2002 show that overall robbery rose 28 per cent to 121,000 incidents.

Dan Munford and Nadine Dorries

3   Home Office recorded crime figures, July 2002 show that the rise in overall robbery figures included a 31 per cent rise in robbery of personal property, most of which are muggings and snatches on the streets.

4   Oliver Letwin, in a speech to the Centre for Policy Studies, 19 June 2002

5   J Graham and B Bowling, *Young People and Crime* (Home Office Research Study 145), Home Office, 1995

6   Speech by the Shadow Home Secretary, Oliver Letwin, to the Centre for Policy Studies (Sixth Keith Joseph Memorial Lecture 2002)

7   Dr Stephen Scott, Department of Child Psychiatry, King's College London, has shown that by the age of five, fifteen per cent of children display early signs of behavioural problems and are rejected by their parents.

8   National Prison Survey 1995, Home Office

9   According to Oliver Letwin's recent speech to the Centre for Policy Studies, within two years of emerging from a young offenders' institution, 75 per cent of leavers will have been reconvicted of a crime.

10   Robert D Putnam, *Bowling Alone: the Collapse and Revival of American Community*, Simon and Schuster, 2000

11   Home Office recorded crime figures, July 2002

12   Robert J Sampson, Stephen Raudenenbush and Felton Earls, 'Crime: A Multi-level Study of Collective Efficacy', *Science*, 15 August 1997, pages 918-924

13   Elijah Anderson, S*treetwise: Race, Class, and Change in an Urban Community*, University of Chicago Press, 1990

14   Sir John Stevens, June 2000 – see also Catriona Marchant, 'Solutions to Youth Crime', *Police Review*, 7 June 2002

15   Dr Michael Schluter is Director of the Cambridge-based Relationships Foundation; from Jonathan Burnside and Nicola Baker (eds), *Relational Justice: Repairing the Breach*, The Relationships Foundation, 1994

16   *The Marketing Pocket Book* (2001 Edition), NTC Publications

17   Robert D Putnam, op. cit.

18   Quotation taken from *Relational Justice: Repairing the Breach*, op. cit.

19   *One parent families today – the facts*, National Council for One Parent Families, September 2001

20   *Teenage Pregnancy*, Social Exclusion Unit, June 1999

21   www.kidsco.org.uk, July 2002

22   'Big noises call for quiet', *Guardian*, 15 November 2000

Nine

Prevention is better than cure

People without hope or a sense of belonging often drift into patterns of anti-social or self-destructive behaviour. Children in this position can find themselves on a fast-moving conveyor belt to crime. Community and charitable institutions are in the best position to address the early causes of social breakdown but government, too, has a role to play. Public policy should intelligently help at-risk groups avoid destructive choices and so build individual and community well-being.

Overleaf Sajid Javid applies this principle to the mounting challenge of personal indebtedness.

Debt and the way we live now

Sajid Javid

Sajid Javid grew up on a working-class estate in Bristol. He was touched by many people whose lives were shattered by excessive personal debt. Sajid now lives in London, working as an investment banker, and is married with two young children.

People's dreams these days are built on hope, hard work – and, often, a mountain of debt. Without loans or credit cards, Clive and Emma Green could not have gone on to higher education or bought and furnished their home in Bristol.

The young couple had amassed £20,000 in student loans and £10,000 in credit card bills by the end of 1998. They thought that they were managing even if merely making the minimum monthly payments. They expected Clive's income to rise in the coming years and so allow them to pay off their debt.

Clive, an insurance salesman, did double his salary. But the Greens found that instead of using their extra income to repay debt, they would just spend more. 'Every time I was say £100 below my credit card limits, Emma and I would just treat ourselves to an expensive dinner or day out with our boys.' Their debt problems compounded when Emma gave up her primary school teaching post to become a full-time mother.

Earlier this year, Clive learnt that his employer had laid off tens of people following a merger with a rival. Many of his friends had lost their jobs but Clive had managed to dodge 'the bullet'. They realised they were on the precipice of debt mountain, and began debt counselling. 'We were so close to losing it all', Clive says.

Before anyone throws stones at the Greens they should consider the glass house they may themselves live in.

Britons today have amassed a record mountain of consumer debt – estimated at over £700 billion (excluding mortgages).[1] That translates to £18,000 per household. Furthermore, this debt mass is growing at the fastest rate in our entire history.

The anonymity of modern debt

Contrary to popular belief, consumer debt is not a modern phenomenon. Starting in the nineteenth century, working people could acquire the then defining symbols of the middle classes – pianos, or sewing machines – on instalment plans. But, back then, you had to go to the vendors of these goods in person to obtain a loan. If you defaulted on the loan, those friendly neighbourhood vendors knew exactly who you were and where you resided. You probably passed them on the street on a daily basis.

Today, virtually anyone over the age of eighteen can purchase almost anything on credit, be it a car, cinema ticket or the weekly shopping. We Britons can get credit at a blink of an eye, over the internet in just a few minutes, without any personal relationship with the lender. What's more, if we default, none of our neighbours need know. Even if they find out, there is no shame or repentance in this era of everyone's-doing-it credit. In the 1950s consumer borrowing was the 'never-never'; in the 1970s it was 'debt'; and now it's called 'credit'. Soon perhaps we'll be calling it 'income'.

Like the Greens, working people are also borrowing more due to general economic optimism. Employment is high, house prices are soaring and interest rates are generally low. People are acting on their impulses. 'There's just something about pulling out that credit card', said Clive Green, 'a complete denial of what's coming.' But acting on impulse is nothing new. What is new is the ease of succumbing to the impulse and the frequency and ingenuity of the ways in which credit is presented to us. Fifty years ago you couldn't walk into a branch of Barclays and demand £100 for a night out and a new pair of shoes. Now, without having to articulate the repayment mechanism, all you have to do is whip out the Barclaycard and the weekend's sorted. Companies are now climbing over themselves to offer you credit; we are offered inducements galore from airline miles to three months' interest free facilities. Just consider the fact that last year alone over 800 million credit card solicitations were mailed out within the UK.[2]

Distressed borrowing

It is not just the financially confident that are whipping out one of their many credit cards. More worryingly, 'the unconfident' are borrowing more and more, too. This includes people without work; people who are too ill to work and people who are suffering from the breakdown of relationships. These people and those on a fragile financial footing are borrowing in greater numbers. These vulnerable individuals, perhaps more than working people, are suffering from the consequences of high personal debt. They not only borrow from the loan sharks but from established licensed lenders. Many find themselves unable to break their addiction to easy credit. But managing debt isn't like controlling most other compulsions. If you're a drinker, you can keep alcohol out of the house. If you're a gambler, you can avoid the trips to the bookies. But if you're a heavy borrower, you don't have to do anything to fall over the precipice because the precipice, in the form of interest on interest, often finds you.

Politicians, of all stripes, have ignored the consumer debt problem. That is a mistake because free-flowing credit often leads to misery and strife. It keeps people awake at night. It contributes to failed relationships and lone parent families; a vast majority of divorced couples say that debt problems played a significant part in the breakdown of their relationship.[3] It leads to crime. On estates like Easterhouse, the police will tell you that after drugs, debt problems are one of the major causes of theft and burglary.[4] Clearly, politicians need to wake up to this growing problem, one that must be dealt with effectively but also compassionately.

This is a particularly important opportunity and responsibility for the Conservative Party. It is an opportunity because the Conservative Party needs to distance itself from our perceived indulgence of business practices – such as long working hours and easy credit – that have hurt vulnerable people. It is a responsibility for the Conservative Party because – like Nixon in China – we are in a better political position to confront big business with the consequences of policies that have led to excessive personal indebtedness. My work at the heart of the City of London makes me an instinctive supporter of market mechanisms. But these should not be unlimited in scope and purpose. There are many potential steps that can be taken by the next Conservative Government to tackle this problem. Michael Howard has already investigated one innovative debt counselling approach provided by a Conservative local authority. I am most committed to similar preventative and early intervention approaches that illustrate that most obvious, but overlooked, of Conservative principles, that prevention is better than cure. But other action is also necessary. I beg readers who disagree with my prescriptions to avoid throwing the baby out with the bath water. There may be better alternatives to my policy ideas but indifference to the debt problem will only exacerbate a human and economic disaster waiting to happen.

Preventing debt problems

First, people should be taught about financial responsibility at an early age. Two-thirds of parents provide children with piggy banks and around fifty per cent have set up bank accounts for their children to encourage financial responsibility.[5] But, away from the home, children receive virtually no formal instruction on financial matters. This is not to suggest that children should sit a GCSE on Prudent Finance but there is a case to teach them about how to manage credit cards and personal finances generally – perhaps in the same way that many schools provide careers guidance. If children knew the difference between APR and CIR, if they could recognise aggressive advertising, if they knew about loan sharks, then maybe, just maybe, they might learn to avoid the climb up debt mountain.

It is not just children that should be taught about financial responsibility. Many adults are financially illiterate. Not because they're not smart – far from it. The financial world has changed dramatically over the last 25 years – presenting individuals with a confusing array of financial products. And in the twenty-first century, you can bet on even more bewildering products. The financially illiterate, not surprisingly, find it difficult to identify the right financial products for themselves and hence fall victim to abusive practices and can respond to financial difficulties in a way that often makes their situation worse.

There is a clear case for better financial education. The Department of Education and Skills and the Financial Services Authority (FSA) should take lead responsibility. But neither of these two bodies should undertake the educational work themselves but should instead cajole financial institutions and empower civil society groups to do so. Special efforts should be made to target help on people vulnerable to indebtedness. Financial management advice should, for example, be focused on high-risk groups like students, families with new babies and people who lose jobs.

More support needs to given to voluntary organisations, such as

There is such a thing as society

Citizens Advice Bureaux, that help the indebted to overcome their problems. Such organisations play a vital role in helping low-income people deal with debt. Many people need advice and information on their legal rights in matters relating to debt consolidation, bailiffs and unscrupulous lenders. They need to know how to deal with and, most importantly, avoid unscrupulous lenders. Whilst some government funding is given to organisations such as CAB more needs to be done. Furthermore, since some lenders are part of the problem, shouldn't they be asked to do more? It's time to consider a small levy on all lenders and organisations that encourage gambling in order to fund the fantastic work of voluntary organisations that assist the indebted. Government should also ensure that private, non-voluntary, debt 'counsellors' are clearly identified. Too many sales people, working for lenders, label themselves 'counsellors' – serving only their own interest.

A preventative approach will also encourage credit unions and other initiatives that help lower-income people build up assets. Credit unions have recently come under the supervision of the FSA and this regime needs to be carefully monitored. Whilst credit unions serve a range of people from different income groups they are particularly active amongst lower-income groups. They do not, however, reach the very poorest people because they often require prior commitment to patterns of saving before granting even the smallest of loans. Active consideration should be given to devolving responsibility for running the Social Fund to any willing credit unions or other charities who could link loans to wider social care or savings projects.

214

Tackling abuses

Secondly, more needs to be done to protect people from abuse. There are far too many people, especially the most vulnerable, who suffer from extortionate interest rates or credit terms that confer an unfair advantage on the lender. Providers of bad debt consolidation loans and those that specialise in lending to low-income groups are often the worst abusers. Iain Duncan Smith learnt about such abusive practices during his visit to Glasgow's Easterhouse estate. The extraordinary commercialisation of Christmas puts enormous pressure on low-income families to provide their children with presents that they cannot afford. Loan sharks seize this opportunity and prey on anxious mums and dads. Small loans can then take much of the following year to repay and make it difficult for families to save for the next Christmas.

Existing legislation on extortionate credit is weighted heavily in favour of lenders. The credit provider can only be challenged by a borrower, at substantial legal costs to the challenger. The system needs to show more compassion. Lending terms need to be transparent. It should be made much easier to challenge lenders (whether as a borrower or a third party) through the courts. Also, in an effort to further shift the balance from lenders to borrowers, perhaps we should introduce the equivalent of 'large print' tobacco-style 'health' warnings on all credit advertising.

Thirdly, the use of distress in debt recovery should be outlawed. There is no question that people who do not repay their debts should be legally forced to do so. Their property must ultimately be made available to lenders. But distress, caused by the use of bailiffs, can have a devastating impact on people's lives. Each year, approximately one million court orders authorising bailiffs are issued.[6] The laws governing the issuing of such orders are complicated and archaic, many dating back over centuries. Most bailiffs are decent people performing a professional and necessary job. But too many bailiffs damage the reputation of the trade and are little more than legalised thugs. They make abusive comments and threaten violence. Many charge inflated collection fees and costs to the distressed debtor. This is not compatible with a modern, compassionate society. The whole system of bailiffs is crying out for root and branch reform.

Cultural attitudes to debt

Perhaps the most important – and yet most difficult – change that we must endeavour to make is in our culture's attitude towards debt. Can we do more to encourage people to avoid 'choosing' debt? Understandably, for many people, debt can appear not to be an 'option' but a 'necessity'. However, as we have seen, for many it is a lifestyle choice and one that can have disastrous consequences.

In some communities debt still has a stigma attached to it and people simply defer consumption as opposed to taking on debt to finance it. In such communities, the natural instinct of people is to turn to their family and friends if they have pressing or economically sound borrowing needs. As a result, while on the one hand repayment terms are more generous and flexible, default rates are extremely low. Let's be frank. If you don't pay your brother back, you'll never hear the end of it. In the UK, many Jewish and Asian households still operate in this manner. I have personal experience of this. Perhaps we can learn from these communities.

We all understand that personal consumption is an important component of the economic well-being of a nation and that the availability of credit is an intrinsic enabler of much economic activity. However, the unbridled growth of consumer credit brings many social problems. There are many obvious steps that can be taken by government to tackle the problems of consumer debt whilst maintaining its liberating value. This goes to the very heart of compassionate conservatism, building a society that promotes freedom and responsibility at the same time. Only that combination will ensure that our advancing economy includes, and protects, vulnerable people.

If you are facing debt challenges yourself or know someone who needs help and advice please contact Credit Action on 0800 591084 or the Consumer Credit Counselling Service on 0800 1381111. Local Citizens Advice Bureaux may also be helpful and can be found via www.nacab.org.uk.

1   BBC News, 30 August 2001

2   BBC News, 20 February 2002

3   *Money in the Contemporary Family*, Bath University, July 2001

4   Avon & Somerset Police Constabulary, July 2002

5   BBC News, 12 July 2001

6   Lord Chancellor's Department, 1998

Ten

Top-down is the wrong way up

Government needs to understand its limits. It lacks the ability to interpret and respond to the volume and complexity of information that is characteristic of a free society. Government must honour the principle of subsidiarity and promote those institutions of society that prosper on a human scale, handing over power to local institutions and frontline professionals. Information on needs and services, and the power to act upon it, is most effectively shared locally rather than through central command systems.

Overleaf Melanie Batley and Peter Franklin apply this principle to a Conservative understanding of wealth redistribution.

A Conservative approach
to redistribution

Peter Franklin and Melanie Malluk Batley

*Peter Franklin is a policy analyst with the social affairs think tank
Renewing One Nation and the editor of* Conservatism *magazine.
He has a background in environmental and rural public policy, and
was one of the founders of a community development project in his
hometown of Edenbridge in Kent.*

*Melanie Malluk Batley is the Work and Pensions Research and
Media Officer at Conservative Central Office, and lives with her
husband in north London. She specialised in urban revitalisation and
economic development for a masters degree at the London School of
Economics. Before moving to Britain, Melanie worked on several
Republican campaigns in the United States.*

Decentralise, devolve, localise, liberate and empower – these are
the watchwords of a new Conservative Party determined to

transform Britain from the bottom up. But don't call it a revolution. As Franz Kafka said, 'every revolution evaporates and leaves behind only the slime of a new bureaucracy.'

Revolutions gather power to themselves. Revolutionaries are the great centralisers and exercisers of power through bureaucracies designed or adapted for that purpose. The Blair revolution may be better known by its four-letter synonym – spin, but is nonetheless effective in taking power from those to whom it might otherwise belong – as our public service professionals know to their cost.

Under the leadership of Iain Duncan Smith, the Conservative Party has realised that the best way to regain power is to promise to give it away again – to individuals, families, communities and institutions. To anyone, it seems, except politicians and the state. And that is an impression that will be seized upon and exploited by those who would rather keep the power where it is.

Few people have a problem with cutting out the state, unless, that is, they are led to believe that it is the same thing as cutting services and support for vulnerable people. In other words, New Labour will do everything it can to steer the Conservative decentralising agenda on to the rocks of redistribution.

Redistribution would appear to be the centralisers' strong suit. On the one hand, redistribution underpins welfare, fairness and social justice. On the other, redistribution represents the ultimate top-down activity, the essence of state power, the *sine qua non* of socialism itself. If the decentralisers are to prevail we must accept the one hand, but reject the other. We can turn the top-down principle on its head and be reconciled to redistribution; indeed it is essential that we must do so.

Conservatives and redistribution

Given its political associations it is unsurprising that Conservative politicians don't like to talk about redistribution. But the truth is they all do it – in government, anyway. Though the tension between cutting taxes and redistributing income is obvious, there is no necessary contradiction in these objectives.

When the Conservatives came to power in 1979 the top rate of income tax was 83 per cent, Geoffrey Howe cut it to sixty per cent and in 1988 Nigel Lawson cut it again to forty per cent. So far, so Tory. But over that time the proportion of income tax contributed by the richest one per cent grew and grew. It was eleven per cent in 1979. It is over twenty per cent now. This phenomenon wasn't limited to the very richest. For instance, the richest ten per cent now contribute half of all income tax revenues.[1] In short, while Labour made the pips squeak louder, the Conservatives were the more accomplished redistributors.

It ought to be obvious that the fundamental question concerning redistribution is not 'how much?' but 'how?'. Less obvious is that this is a two-part question – with a 'supply side' (i.e. how we raise the taxes) and a 'demand side' (i.e. how we allocate the proceeds). The supply side is well-trodden ground, watered by a regular flow of ingenious taxation schemes. However, the demand side is all but overlooked.

Trickledown welfare

We are now all too familiar with the left wing critique of 'trickledown economics' – that is the idea that burgeoning wealth in higher income groups will make its way down to lower income groups via free market mechanisms. The concern is not just whether trickledown actually happens, but whether it demeans the poor even if it does. This is puzzling, because most left-wingers have no problem with 'trickledown welfare' – that is the idea that tax revenues should be poured out from vast government budgets, nourishing enormous bureaucracies as they flow through top-down distribution mechanisms only to be received as a thin stream of dependency by vulnerable individuals at the bottom end.

Perhaps we should not be puzzled for long; after all, the parties of the Left exist to represent the interests of those whose power and position depend upon this mode of redistribution. The great challenge and opportunity for the Conservative Party is to distinguish this interest from the interests of the legitimate recipients and providers of welfare.

The funding jungle

State funding of the voluntary sector is a good place to get started. By the Government's own estimate, the state provides £5 billion in public funds to the voluntary sector every year.[2] For the most part this is distributed through grant and contract mechanisms of staggering complexity and incoherence.

To get some idea of the sheer density of the funding jungle, David Willetts, Shadow Secretary of State for Work and Pensions, asked the House of Commons Library to work out how many area-based initiatives to help regenerate poor communities were in current operation by the Government. The answer was thirty different schemes of which up to 21 were operating concurrently in each of Britain's ten most deprived wards. Willetts makes clear what this means in practical terms:

> All around the country decent people who want to be running youth clubs or caring for elderly people are instead putting all their time and energy into filling out pages and pages of forms to bid for penny packets of money under some special scheme. Our hard-pressed communities are often desperately short of dedicated people, volunteers or professionals, who will give their time and effort. The last thing they need is such an enormous diversion of their energies into this extraordinary time-consuming and dispiriting process.[3]

However, it is not just the waste and the exclusion of smaller community groups that matter. A funding system controlled by politicians and bureaucrats distorts the priorities of those voluntary organisations that depend on it. According to the National Council for Voluntary Organisations the voluntary sector receives thirty per cent of its income from the state[4] and some major charities are now almost entirely funded from the public purse.[5] This raises immediate concerns over political and bureaucratic interference in the sector, which have been variously expressed by the socialist neighbourhood worker Bob Holman,[6] the pioneering social entrepreneur Andrew Mawson,[7] the Liberal Democrat peer Lord Dahrendorf[8] and, on behalf of Britain's faith communities, Steve Chalke, who heads up the Faithworks campaign.[9]

And yet public funding *per se* is not the problem. The problem is when decision-making structures allow politicians to control public money as an agent of transmission for the values, practices and structures of the state. The solution is to turn those structures upside down, creating funding mechanisms that empower donors, volunteers, providers and recipients. A very simple example is the Gift Aid system, which allows charities to reclaim tax on donations. At the time of writing, 28 pence is refunded for every pound donated. An increase in that rate could be used to channel public funds to charities currently distributed by other means. In theory, the state could rely on this method alone for distributing funds to the voluntary sector. Of course, this would be unacceptably simplistic. But it is a moot point as to whether such a means of allocating resources would be any more inefficient and unjust than the waste, bureaucracy and politicisation of the current system.

Fortunately, these are not the only options. There are a variety of other bottom-up funding mechanisms available. Realistic solutions will emerge from a mix of innovative approaches. The NCVO's interest in local charitable endowments is worthy of consideration. Voucher systems where money follows the individual in need would potentially lead to more diverse social provision. How other countries incentivise charitable giving – particularly corporate philanthropy – should be studied. Delegated or intermediary-based systems of accreditation and audit could expand the pool of funded organisations. Schemes matching funding to an organisation's success in motivating volunteers and attracting private funding could be expanded. Having experienced the high-handed insensitivity of bureaucracies to local needs, Bob Holman suggests that public funds be channelled to resident-controlled community projects by elected neighbourhood trusts.[10] Of course, it is not a case of singling out any one of these ideas for general application, but rather of planting the right mechanism in the right place, standing back and allowing its bottom-up nature to get on with it.

But while £5 billion is a lot of money, state funding of the voluntary sector is only the start of reforming redistribution. Much greater amounts are redistributed through the state education system, the NHS, social services departments and other organs of the welfare state. How can we apply the bottom-up principle in this arena? The answer is that this should happen automatically as a result of pursuing a wider agenda of decentralisation within the public services. There are many good reasons for respecting the autonomy and authority of public service professionals, just as there are for giving public service users more choice, but a necessary side-effect of either, or rather, both, would be to wrest control of public funding streams from state power structures. A genuine dialogue between public service providers free to decide what to provide and public service users free to decide what to use leaves little role for politicians except to decide overall funding levels – broad enough an issue to settle at the ballot box (along with how the money is raised).

Welfare as if people mattered

However, what is true for the public services, the providers of 'welfare in kind', is not true for the benefits system, the provider of 'cash welfare'. Though complex in the extreme, the benefits system has no equivalent of the autonomous public service professions such as nursing or teaching – nor do we find public service institutions like schools and hospitals between which users can make a meaningful choice. How then can we hope to overturn top-down control of this purest form of redistribution?

First let us consider how the benefits system treats people: lose your job, and report to the local Jobcentre agency for an application for Jobseeker's Allowance. Complete a form and take a number. Wait on the plastic-covered metal connected chairs in a room with a dirty carpet, few windows, and dozens of other people who will be called before you. Reading material includes nicely printed government brochures with smiling people on the front. When your number is called, report to the glass window and answer courteous questions about the factual details on the application. After 21 days, if you're applying at the Euston benefit office, for example, you will receive your giro.

As a social safety net, this welfare arrangement works for a person who may have unexpectedly lost their job (except for those who lose their job on the first and whose rent is due on the fifteenth). But in a vast number of cases, circumstances aren't as tidy. Problems with alcohol and drugs, family breakdown, crime, homelessness, and individual isolation all play a role, and receiving money from the benefit office just helps to pay the bills. Yet, every year, the House convenes a debate on the level of benefit increases. Gordon Brown busily tinkers with his system of 'tax credits', (a term used to disguise increased benefit spending, both politically and financially), as diligent civil servants pore over their computer screens in the Treasury to fine-tune ever more intricate adjustments to the incomes of millions of people.[11]

But, the flaw in the liberal view of welfare provision is that it doesn't do enough. It rests on the assumption that deprivation is fundamentally a matter of finances, and that whichever party is willing to give more money is the more compassionate party. It doesn't address the problems that underlie the causes of need. Poverty is as much an aspirational, relational and intensely individual problem as it is financial and economic. Bureaucratic government programmes and the lady sitting behind the glass in the Jobcentre are simply not in a position to address the unique circumstances that lead people to a life of need; they are alien to the people they're trying to help.

If we are truly concerned with empowering people, then the benefits system and associated social services must be focused on lifting people into a position in which they can be in control of their own fates. The system should reflect Beveridge's model of a social safety net: it would be there for you if you need it, but would have incentives to help you get back to the life you want as quickly as possible. As Beveridge argued:

> The state in organising security should not stifle incentive, opportunity, responsibility; in establishing a national minimum, it should leave room and encouragement for voluntary action by each individual to provide more than that minimum for himself and his family.'[12]

Under the current system of centralised welfare provision, tackling poverty and empowering people is simply unachievable, while the voluntary organisations that are designed to reach individuals one-by-one are often shut out. But what if when people came into benefit offices, they were given 'not a list of goods and services that government offers, but a list of groups, from various religions and ideologies, to which they can be connected?'[13] This could apply to all services like drug treatment, homeless programs, housing, and juvenile programmes. The government would change from a dictator to a facilitator, linking people in need with programmes of their choice, some of which may be located right in their own neighbourhoods.

We've already argued that the top-down approach to redistribution should be overturned in cases of direct state funding for voluntary groups. But the same principle could be applied to benefit recipients to give them control over the use of funds that the Government would otherwise be spending on their behalf. For example, there are many benefits which provide money for particular purposes, such as housing, childcare and employment training. These need to become more flexible so that individuals can use those funds to finance whichever programme provides them and their families with the best chance of achieving financial independence from the state.

The faultline

We have reached a stage where it has become absolutely critical for Conservatives to win the argument on benefit provision, because since 1997, millions more people have been pulled into the system who have never before had any contact with it. In Gordon Brown's last Budget speech, he set out the new thresholds for receipt of government funds. The new Child Tax Credit will apply to all families with salaries up to £58,000 or less. Those earning £50,000 or less will receive £1,400 per year or

£26.50 per week. Those earning between £50,000 and £58,000 will receive between £800 and £1,400 per year.[14]

Labour is doing this for a reason. The increase in means-tested benefits[15] not only forces more people to rely on the state who never before had to, but it also erodes incentives to make or save more money. Gordon Brown should put his mouth where our money is. He should admit what his actions suggest, which is that he believes himself better qualified to decide how other people's money is spent than the people themselves.

While Brown has been busy extending his grip on higher incomes, we should not forget that it is the poorest people who have the least control over their incomes. Labour's move to manage the incomes of those well into the top rate income tax bracket is absurd and must be reversed. But the real challenge is to find ways of giving everyone control over their incomes whether supported through redistribution or otherwise.

We are the only party that believes that the people, not politicians, should be in charge of their lives in this way. This is what we want for everyone – people living on low incomes and people hit by life shocks like redundancy, as well as the millions of ordinary families pushed by Brown into his 'tax credit' system for the first time. It is essential that we find a way to communicate our vision to the people, and to explain why the Government's approach is misguided. After all, it is on this issue that the real fault line runs between New Labour and today's Conservatives.

There is such a thing as society

Conclusion

Redistribution is an ugly word for a noble instinct. Even uglier is the tendency of politicians to use top-down systems of redistribution to exploit the civilising desire of societies to share their wealth. In this country we do not tolerate office holders who skim public funds for financial gain, but for too long we have allowed them to extract all the power and influence generated by a stream of money and hold it back for political gain. It is a power that should be used by public service professionals, by voluntary organisations, by communities, families and individuals. It is a means of empowerment by which vulnerable people might become less so. And, as such, it is a resource, which justly shared out, might just allow society to reduce the amount of wealth it needs to redistribute – but for the best and most sustainable of reasons.

1   James Bartholomew, *Daily Telegraph*, 24 January 2001
2   Angela Eagle, *Hansard*, column 703W, 30 April 2002 – though an increasing tax burden means that much of this goes straight back to the Treasury.
3   David Willetts, in a speech delivered to Renewing One Nation, 27 February 2002
4   *Voluntary Sector Almanac 2002*, National Council for Voluntary Organisations
5   Robert Whelan et al, *Involuntary Action*, IEA Health and Welfare Unit, 1999
6   Ibid.
7   Charles Leadbeater, *The Rise of the Social Entrepreneur*, Demos, 1997
8   Lord Dahrendorf, 'Challenges to the Voluntary Sector', Arnold Goodman Lecture, 17 July 2001
9   Steve Chalke, 'Faithworks', Kingsway, April 2001
10 Robert Whelan et al, op. cit.
11 David Willetts, op. cit.

Peter Franklin and Melanie Malluk Batley

William Beveridge, *Social Insurance and Allied Services*, Cmd. 6404, 1942
13 Marvin Olasky, *Compassionate Conservatism*, The Free Press, 2000, page 175
14 *The 2002 Financial Statement and Budget Report*, HM Treasury
15 Means-tested benefits are benefits that are determined by a person's level of income, so that the less you earn or save, the more you receive.

Eleven

Change the culture, not just the law

Abuse of certain social and economic freedoms, that government is ill-equipped to regulate, can lead to acute human misery. Borrowing incautiously, reckless speculation and excessive working hours are examples. Compassionate Conservatives will promote responsible exercise of these freedoms but not always through legislation and regulation. Political leadership should transcend the apparatus of the state and provide a strong voice for the common good in the culture.

Overleaf Fiona Bruce applies this principle to the issue of working hours.

Defeating the
long-hours culture

Fiona Bruce

Fiona Bruce has practised as a solicitor for over twenty years. In 1988 she founded the Warrington law firm Fiona Bruce & Co, which today has over ten solicitors and some thirty staff. In 1993 the firm was the first sole-practitioner law firm to gain the Investors In People award. Fiona writes and speaks widely on behalf of the National Law Society on workplace management. She lives in Cheshire with her husband and their two young sons.

What do we want from our politicians? Obviously, we elect Members of Parliament to legislate on our behalf. But we also look to them for leadership and direction – inevitably so because they are in the public eye. Not only for that reason, though. There is a deeply felt desire within people to be led by men and women who are confident of their own direction and who demonstrate this by how they live as well as by what they say. Leaders who, by their own example, inspire each of us to reach beyond our natural abilities and expectations to achieve in ways which make a real and genuine contribution to the common good.

We don't live our lives in a vacuum, but in a culture where all sorts of external influences shape the way we live. The media, big business, pressure groups and unions – countless competing interests seek to impose their agendas on us every day. No one can doubt that these voices can and do change the way we live. But all too often the voice that speaks for the good of the whole nation is silent. If the Conservative Party wants to be listened to again it must start providing that voice. We should challenge the sectional interests and lead change that it is in the common interest. Let us begin with an aspect of our national culture on which people may be surprised to hear us speak – the long-hours culture.

Working hours in Britain today

The British now work the longest hours in Europe – an average of 8.7 hours daily, compared to 7.9 in France and 8.0 in Germany.[1] The PSI/LSE 'Working in Britain' survey found that one in three male employees, and one in ten female employees, work over fifty hours a week.[2] These are the sort of statistics that normally pave the way to a call for more regulation, but here's another statistic worth taking into account: The Forum of Private Business estimates that an average of over ten hours a week, much of it at evenings and weekends, is spent by small business owners, on regulatory compliance, before they can even begin their remunerated work.[3] More regulation is not a panacea. Politicians need to realise that they can't always change the world at the stroke of a legislative pen. On the balance between life and work, as with so many other issues, we need to start thinking about changing the culture, not the law.

There are many reasons why so many people work such long hours. Some, like the employers referred to above, are obliged to. Others feel they are obliged to – some motivated by the best of reasons – such as commitment, duty, and a positive work ethic. However, for many people the reasons are less positive: they include fear of redundancy; increased competitiveness; a desire to exhibit the 'macho image' of sustaining work at both high pressure and high speed; a misplaced sense of self-worth derived from the illusion that we are indispensable; and, of course, increased material expectations. All of these have added to the time we spend at, and travelling to and from, work.

Consequences and costs

Whatever the reasons, one thing is clear. We are not happy with these working hours, and neither are our minds, nor our bodies. The 'Working in Britain' survey found that in 2000 only 24 per cent of us were happy with our working hours – a reduction from 44 per cent in 1992.[4] We are suffering increasing levels of stress, worry, and depression. A recent study of over 700 men concluded that those who worked over sixty hours a week and slept for an average of five hours or less each night had twice the risk of a heart attack as those working up to forty hours a week.[5] Earlier and earlier retirement, often due to 'burn out', means the loss from businesses and professions of a wealth of accumulated wisdom and experience. All of us are bearing the extra tax costs imposed as a result of increasingly burdened health and social security services.

Family relationships are paying a huge price. I work as a solicitor in a high street law firm in the North West. The one area of our firm's work which has grown out of all proportion during the last decade, without any endeavours to promote it on our part, is divorce work. We would rather this were not so. According to the charity Young Voice, almost one quarter of fourteen- to eighteen-year olds say their parents are too stressed to have any time for them.[6] Dr Howard Steele, a University of London psychologist, found that very young children, deprived of quality time with their fathers, (such as their regular presence at evening bath time), are ten times more likely to suffer emotional damage than other children.[7] Long working days combined with increased commuting hours mean that many families rarely meet together from one weekend to the next, and even then, many pass each other fleetingly; and rarely eat together. A study of 12,000 US students found that many teenage problems, particularly drug abuse, are significantly less likely in families where parents and children eat together in the evening.[8]

There is such a thing as society

Not only are our family relationships suffering, but also our wider community relationships. Often, we barely know our neighbours. Local charities find it increasingly difficult to attract volunteers. So the relationships which oil the wheels of our community infrastructures are absent, or are so superficial as to make no meaningful difference to our lives when life shocks strike.[9]

Political involvement – pertinent or impertinent?

Do we need to work such long hours? Could we as a nation be more productive and fulfilled if we reduced them? Why do we work in this way and how could government help facilitate a change to less demanding work patterns? Indeed are these questions which politicians should be asking at all? The compassionate Conservative answer to this question must be 'yes!'

Some would argue that working hours are a matter of private contractual agreement between employees and employers. But how many millions of people actually work the hours specified in their employment contracts? How many people actually need to work the hours that they do? What is the true cost of Britain's work–life imbalance and who picks up the bill? And, finally, if we believe that children are entitled to their parents' love and attention, how can we just leave the issue of working hours to the market place where children cannot compete for their parents' time?

Looking at these issues goes to the heart of what good government is about: promoting and facilitating the complete well-being of a nation.

More regulation is not the answer

Perhaps Conservatives would be right not to ask questions about working hours if the only answer was more regulation. A decent degree of protection is required in the law, but we must also understand the diminishing returns of ever-increasing regulation. Take the Working Time Directive for instance, what impact has that made on Britain's long-hours culture? The unions argue that it is more vigorously enforced in other EU countries. But they do not take into account increased levels of short-term contract and black market employment which leave workers even more vulnerable to exploitation. Then, as the Forum of Private Business points out, regulatory compliance puts a terrible burden on the working hours of employers and self-employed people in small businesses. Indeed, more regulation could result in many employers quitting the employment market altogether. In doing so, they would contribute to higher levels of unemployment and exacerbate the time imbalance between those in work, and those who have no work at all. In a saner world working hours would be more evenly spread through the population. But can we expect small businesses to deliver sanity if we drive them up the wall with employment regulations?

Beyond regulation

For a sustainable solution, we need to look beyond regulation. We need to change the long-hours culture, because that's just what it is – a culture. And like any culture it has low and high aspects. For an example of the former, just think how many office workers find themselves hanging about at the end of the day for no better reason than not wanting to be first out the door. As for the latter, why is it that in many professions long hours are a symbol of status and success?

We could choose to live life differently. Consider the lives of one family I know well: Margaret has six children, including two adopted daughters, and is a foster mother. She and her husband Peter, who is a painter and decorator, have never had a lot of money. In all the fifteen years or so I have known them the family have never gone abroad for a holiday. But they always have a smile on their faces, and are fit and well. Peter ensures that whatever the job he is working on, he is always home for the family's evening meal. Their welcoming home is always full of happiness and fun. Their children have wonderfully developed musical and sporting skills, well-rounded personalities and are pursuing interesting lives, in which their parents remain involved.

This is what Margaret says:

> Our society is wrong when it says that children want designer clothes, PlayStations, etc. What children want is a relationship with their parents. They want their parents to listen to them. Children want parents to be interested in their lives. They want to sit round a table at night and tell their Mum what has gone on during the day.

My guess is that at the end of their lives Peter and Margaret will be two of the most fulfilled people I know. In my eyes they will also be two of the most successful – defined not in material terms, but in having fulfilled their life potential, enjoyed life's journey on the way, and having done so through concentrating on giving out to others, rather than on acquiring, in life. Contrast Peter and Margaret with the 'thirty-somethings' interviewed for a survey commissioned by Virgin One Account. This found that a third of respondents were 'in the depths of a classic mid-life crisis'; felt they weren't making the most of life; felt trapped by financial commitments and mounting responsibilities; and were swamped by feelings of panic.[10] In short, they wanted to stop the world and get off.

What can politicians do?

A key starting point is to raise awareness – by being bold enough to open up discussion in the political arena. Bold, because these have not been areas touched upon by Conservative politicians over recent generations. Needless to say, cries of 'nanny state!' or 'living others' lives for them!' or 'judgemental!' will be heard. But compassionate Conservatives should press on regardless. In opening up this debate we open up the options for people to consider how they can live more fulfilled lives, freed from the constricting conformity which conventional working patterns impose.

On winning the leadership of the Conservative Party, Iain Duncan Smith said: 'The Party I want to lead will be an effective Opposition to this Government. It will campaign on the issues that matter to people, the core things that affect them most in their daily lives.'[11] There are few issues that affect people more in their daily lives than working hours. Voters will be more interested in hearing what politicians have to say on this than on Europe and the constitution, or, for that matter, the various 'Westminster village' causes that some would have the Conservative Party adopt.

Starting a national debate is the first step to changing a national culture. But politicians should 'walk the talk' too. Leading by example, they should grasp the nettle and change their own working hours. A study by Ashley Weinberg, a psychology lecturer at Salford University, looking at the health of 64 newly elected MPs after the 1997 Election, found that nearly a third experienced exhaustion. Weinberg says: 'In the survey we found the main issue for MPs was balancing work and home life, as most were working 55 to 70 hours a week'.[12] Politicians need to put their own house in order and Conservatives should lead the way.

There are other ways of sending a message without resorting to the blunderbuss of regulation. There are some high-profile companies which almost revel in a long-hours culture. I am not saying that these should be named and shamed. Rather, politicians should keep their distance and give their attention to 'naming and proclaiming' the family-friendly policies of responsible companies. Indeed government should be co-operating with employers on working hours. Examples of best practice should be documented and then actively promoted, just as training has been encouraged through schemes like Investors in People. For its part, government must look at how taxation,

National Insurance and regulation affect employment decisions. In particular, it must remove financial disincentives to employing more people working shorter hours, as opposed to fewer people working longer hours.

Politicians should also combat the myth that the long-hours culture is necessarily good for 'Great Britain Ltd'. For instance, while we work longer hours than our European counterparts, worker productivity in France and Germany is greater than in Britain. Nor do long hours explain the success of the 'Anglo-Saxon model' of capitalism. For while we share a long hours culture with America we also share it with Japan, where they even have a word, *karoshi*, for 'committing suicide by working yourself to death'. In part, the decade-long depression of the Japanese economy was caused by consumers working too hard to enjoy themselves. In short, there are real and tangible benefits to both individual businesses and the whole economy from a workforce which is physically well, not unhealthily stressed, which has time for enjoyable leisure activities and whose personal relationships are sound. Furthermore, a contented workforce is less likely to move on, saving major recruitment and re-training costs. This last point is especially important in a high-employment economy such as Britain's.

Family-friendly hours work

Employers need to develop flexibility and work with their employees to get work–life balances right on a one-to-one basis. Within my solicitors' firm, we have several employees working a variety of hours, mainly to ensure that they can be with their families when their children need them at home. And so, one of the ways in which we have changed our culture over the past few years is by the development of non-confrontational workplace reviews – a world apart from the dreaded appraisal. For the first hour of the review the primary role of the manager is to listen. The review also includes open questions such as:

1   'What are some of the things people do which hinder you from being most effective, and how could we help you to work more effectively?'
2   'How could we help to reduce pressure on you?'
3   'How could you enjoy your work more?'

As a result of management and staff openly discussing their particular pressures, a better understanding has developed over time as to how we can begin to work together to better manage our working hours. For instance we have one member of staff who finishes three days a week at 3.15pm for the school run while another works half a week; we have a grandmother who works short-time during school holidays to help care for her grandchildren and a secretary who knows that whenever she needs to vary her hours to care for her elderly husband she can do so. We also have job share arrangements. As for retirement arrangements, why do so many people have to retire at a set age, and go from long hours straight to no hours? Many older employees would prefer to scale down their hours gradually – we have a number of employees who work on this basis. They are mature and stable members of staff whom we wouldn't be without. Some people might say that such 'outside the box' thinking isn't possible in most workplaces. As an employer, I thought so too – until I tried it! In fact, we now find that not only is it possible, even in a relatively small business, but preferable, bearing in mind the goodwill and flexibility generated. For instance, staff are happy to provide holiday or sickness cover when needed, even at short notice.

But what about the boss? Well, for years now, I have picked my children up from school at the end of the school day, on at least three afternoons a week, most weeks. This means I simply have to leave the office at three o'clock. Amazingly, the business has not collapsed around my feet! In fact, during these years it has continued to grow and develop. And not one of my thirty or so staff believe that I will be impressed if they are still there at eight o'clock at night. For a start, I am not there to see it! I have two boys, aged nine and six. It is good for me to keep reminding myself that they only have one childhood and it is happening now.

Conclusion

My experience is that family-friendly businesses can prosper even within those industries and professions most associated with the long-hours culture. But what about employees trapped in a less flexible work environment? I have already said that they and their children should be protected by the law. But we must ensure that those laws target specific abuses rather than impose a blanket burden on all employers regardless of their record. The long-hours culture cannot and should not be overcome by means that create a no-hours culture of mass unemployment, as in some European countries. Indeed it is in a full-employment economy that a family-friendly culture has the best chance of taking root, because it is family-friendly businesses that would most effectively recruit and retain loyal and contented personnel. One possible model for better regulation has been developed by the Relationships Foundation in the form of the Family Days Protection Bill, which would put an obligation on employers not to employ parents of school-age children over both days of the weekend, other than in exceptional circumstances. This would give families the chance to spend at least one day a week together, without generating onerous bureaucracy for employers.

Where we do resort to a change in the law we need to look beyond its letter and to its spirit. What message does it send out? What is its symbolic importance? Have our elected representatives merely changed the law or have they changed the culture too? The greatest changes in our national life are rarely brought about by the law alone – if at all, but by a change in the attitudes, hopes and aspirations of millions of people. Ultimately we have to choose to change. We need to believe that our choices can make a difference. Let's, for our own and our families' benefit, as our children would say, get a life! Put another way, 'what does it profit a man if he gains the whole world and loses his own soul?'[13] The same could be said of a nation.

And a nation needs leadership. The challenge for Conservatives is to communicate to people that we care about all aspects of their lives, not just the economic.

1   The Centre for Economics and Business Research, April 2002

2   Policy Studies Institute/London School of Economics, *Working in Britain*, quoted in *Working Capital*, The Work Foundation, April 2002

3   The Forum of Private Business, *2002 Red Tape Survey*, May 2002

4   Policy Studies Institute/London School of Economics, op. cit.

5   Y Liu and H Tanaka, 'Overtime work, insufficient sleep, and risk of non-fatal acute myocardial infarction in Japanese men', Occupational and Environmental Medicine, July 2002

6   'Stressed parents failing teenagers', *Observer*, 21 April 2002

7   'New 'Bathtime with Babies' Study Shows Importance of Dads To Children', Fathers Direct, 7 November 2001

8   According to an analysis of the National Longitudinal Study of Adolescent Health conducted by Dr. Kathleen Mullin Harris, of the University of North Carolina, adolescents who share five to seven dinner meals a week with their parents – regardless of family structure – are less likely to participate in substance abuse or early sexual activity; see Anita M Smith, *A simple place to start – the dinner table*, Institute of Youth Development, 2000

9   Robert D Putnam, *Bowling Alone: the Collapse and Revival of American Community*, Simon and Schuster, 2000

10 Virgin One survey reported in 'Cold Feet generation – one in three plunge into midlife crisis in their 30s', *Daily Mail,* 13 July 2002

11 Iain Duncan Smith, 13 September 2001

12 Greg Power (ed), *Under Pressure: Are we getting the most from our MPs?*, Hansard Society, 2000

13 For one of the most penetrating and practical analyses of the work–life balance issue, see *59 minutes to a calmer life* (ISBN: 0953728439) by the leading business training consultant, Paul McGee.

Twelve

Don't take prosperity for granted

Britain's economic renaissance – started in 1979 – provides the hard-won basis for today's opportunities for social renewal. Economic security enables individual flourishing and general well-being. Sustained economic growth creates breathing space for sectional interests to coexist and even be reconciled. Government policy must never imperil the competitive environment upon which much of a 'one nation' agenda depends.

Overleaf Clifford Herbertson applies this principle to the extension of economic opportunity to the poorest people and the need for more competition amongst big business.

Sustaining a purposeful prosperity

Clifford Herbertson

Clifford Herbertson was born in Glasgow and raised in East Kilbride. He and his wife Julie have three boys. As a management consultant, Clifford has worked with a number of the world's largest multinationals in the UK, Europe, North America and Asia. He is currently Group Strategy Director for Exel, the global logistics and supply chain management company.

Prosperity with a purpose

This book and its title will be read by many as a repudiation of the Thatcher years. But Oliver Letwin's essay demonstrates that there is no contradiction between Iain Duncan Smith's mission to renew society and Margaret Thatcher's premiership. Her economic policies of 1979–86, in particular, laid the foundation for the opportunities that every British Government has since enjoyed but which have largely been squandered.

Clifford Herbertson

George W Bush's great criticism of Bill Clinton's presidency was that he had frittered away America's prosperity. Bush told the 2000 Republican Convention:

> Times of plenty, like times of crisis, are tests of American character. Prosperity can be a tool in our hands – used to build and better our country. Or it can be a drug in our system – dulling our sense of urgency, of empathy, of duty. Our opportunities are too great, our lives too short, to waste this moment. So tonight we vow to our nation... We will seize this moment of American promise. We will use these good times for great goals. We will confront the hard issues – threats to our national security, threats to our health and retirement security – before the challenges of our time become crises for our children. And we will extend the promise of prosperity to every forgotten corner of this country. To every man and woman, a chance to succeed. To every child, a chance to learn. To every family, a chance to live with dignity and hope.[1]

At the time of writing, George W Bush is struggling to maintain confidence in the US economy so that it continues to generate the wealth that his programme of compassionate conservatism requires. Bush understands the warning given by Edward Heath to Conservative workers in 1973:[2]

There is such a thing as society

> The alternative to economic expansion is not, as some
> occasionally seem to suppose, an England of quiet
> market towns linked only by trains puffing slowly and
> peacefully through green meadows. The alternative is
> slums, dangerous roads, old factories, cramped schools,
> stunted lives.

The economic growth of the Thatcher years was vital to prevent
that dystopia feared by Heath and it will be necessary to
underpin the radical agenda set out in the essays of this book.
Building and maintaining a strong economy is critical to helping
those people who will always need special care – young children,
the severely disabled, the seriously ill, and the very old. It will
also be more difficult to guarantee the often initially expensive
investment required to help capable vulnerable people move
towards independence.

In assessing how Labour has managed the prosperity it
inherited, Gordon Brown's economic record appears mixed.
Building on the evolutionary changes introduced by Kenneth
Clarke, the decision to grant independence to the Bank of
England laid the foundations for the monetary stability enjoyed
over recent years.[3] Brown's repayment of much of the national
debt has contributed towards his reputation for prudence. But in
at least two key areas of policy Labour is undermining the
economy and society's potential to sustain care for vulnerable
people. Firstly, the Chancellor's imprudent extension of means-
testing has greatly increased dependence upon the state. The fact

that he has extended welfare during prosperous times only intensifies the difficulties that future Chancellors may face at the bottom of an economic cycle. Secondly, there has been a massive and stealthy growth of red tape. The immediate cost implications for business have been well documented; less well observed has been the long-term implications for the structure of economic relations within Britain. The rest of this essay will briefly examine how a future Conservative Government might reverse these two threats to our economic and social security.

Opportunity for 'hard-to-employ' people

The economic growth of the 1980s enabled most people to improve their economic circumstances. But many people without the same levels of capability or self-motivation – and whose family or community situations may have been severely limiting – were left behind. The rising tide of prosperity did not lift these boats because the boats were broken. Broken because of drug addiction or a lifetime's experience of rejection. Broken because the values of work, thrift and responsibility had not been passed from one generation to the next. Broken because of the sheer accumulation of such difficulties in certain hard-pressed areas. This book has documented how community-based institutions are best placed to help vulnerable people build so-called soft skills. They succeed because they are often the only 'professional' presence in disadvantaged areas and because they are committed to a level of personal care that hard-to-employ people need.

There is such a thing as society

On a second visit to Easterhouse, Iain Duncan Smith heard how one young man was helped by the FARE charity.[4] When the young man first came to FARE he couldn't even keep appointments. He had no concept of commitment because he'd never known any himself. He had become unsure of himself in a world that had never taken the trouble to get to know him. When he spoke he couldn't make eye contact but watched his own fidgeting feet. People in the project – free from a mindset that reduced this young man to a target – took the time to befriend him. And it was a lot of time. But they discovered he had a talent. This talent would never win glittering prizes but it provided him with a source of self-worth for the first time in his life. Today that young man has a spring in his step. There's a sparkle in his eyes when he talks to people. He's ready to be a citizen.

The challenge for Conservatives must be to extend opportunity and encouragement to every person like that young man. And we must realise that it won't be cheap in the immediate term. But it is an approach very different from Labour's, as David McLetchie MSP made clear in a speech to Scottish Conservatives.[5] McLetchie warned that Labour's emphasis on means-tested help from remote welfare bureaucracies will not, ultimately, succeed and represents a tragic waste of today's prosperity:

> Through its tax credit policy [Labour] is drawing many
> families, that are by no means poor, into welfare depend-

ency. The new Child Tax Credit goes up the income scale to £58,000 – even more than an MSP earns if such a thing were possible. This is storing up trouble for a time when the economy is on a downturn. It's like building houses with no roofs and hoping that the sun will never stop shining and it limits the ability of the state to help those in real need during bad times. A sensible welfare policy will use today's economic prosperity to encourage sustainable families and to build self-supporting communities. Only then will Scotland be prepared for rainy days'.

In his essay on Kent County Council's 'Supporting Independence' Programme, Sandy Bruce-Lockhart shows how a Conservative local authority is investing today's wealth to reduce dependency. Sandy Bruce-Lockhart and David McLetchie share the straightforward view that it is better to teach a person to fish than to keep feeding him or her with fish. The hard-to-employ people who are the focus of the Kent project are the reason for the failure of what Professor Laurence Mead describes as 'progressive politics':[6]

> The traditional left and right shared the assumption that the individual is willing and able to advance his or her own economic interests. Not just the businessperson, but the ordinary citizen is a maximiser, seeking not just survival, but advancement, in material terms.

The assumption of economic rationality led policy-makers of Left and Right to remove barriers, and raise inducements, to work. Tax credits, childcare provision and training programmes have helped many people but they have not reached the hard-to-employ. An awareness of the limitations of 'progressive politics' should not lead to its wholesale rejection. It still has a role to play but it is not enough. It would also be wrong for government to conclude that it has no responsibility for ensuring the hard-to-employ receive soft skills. It cannot simply abandon people to the care of a still immature community- and faith-based sector.

Faith and community-based ministries help individual people to develop relationship skills but they often lack the connections to the job market that will provide their newly able 'clients' with an opportunity to get meaningful and rewarding work. In *Transforming Charity*,[7] Ryan Streeter identifies the need for integration between soft-skill providers and job providers as a priority for public policy:

> If poverty is as much a moral as an economic issue, then neither the government, nor the business, nor the non-profit sectors can address it by themselves. The success of our future efforts to solve the root causes of poverty will depend upon how well we identify the key responsibilities of each sector and how well they work together, not on the relegation of full responsibility from one sector to another.

Clifford Herbertson

The management of this integration should not follow one blueprint but should be locally-based; reflecting joint decisions by voluntary sector groups, businesses and elected officials. Such integration will serve other purposes, too. It will provide community-based groups with access to general expertise that they lack and should improve their accountability structures. Integration should also ensure that no one falls between gaps in provision. Streeter proposes ServiceMaster[8] as a good example of how a relatively large but devolved business can help soft-skill providers to fulfil their clients' potential. Over the last decade, ServiceMaster is one of a growing number of businesses that help poor communities to organise themselves into revenue-generating enterprises. The community-based organisations help hard-to-employ people to develop a respect for authority, conflict-resolution skills and other attributes and then present them with opportunities in landscaping, house-keeping and the delivery of other customer services. ServiceMaster helps to resource and find customers for these services.

Once vulnerable people are on the road to independence we need to strongly incentivise the opportunities for them to build a lasting stake in society. Conservatives may not be able to present another 'big new idea' like council house sales to the electorate but lots of smaller ideas should contribute to the same goal of empowering poor families. These ideas should focus on the further encouragement of home ownership, savings and asset development, school vouchers and micro-credit facilities to support very small community-based businesses. Any ability we have to grant tax cuts – an agenda that will become much more popular and necessary as the economy weakens – should be used to support the 'renewal of society' mission. A future Conservative government may even decide to redistribute the tax burden – without necessarily cutting it – in favour of families, charitable-giving, saving and small businesses.

There is a real urgency to this task. The longer perfectly able people stay dependent on the state the more they are consuming resources that could be used to improve the life of more vulnerable citizens. The dependency culture also does nothing to break the vicious circle of unemployment, crime, drugs and hopelessness that too many people find themselves trapped inside.

But this section's emphasis on preparing hard-to-employ people for the job market will be pointless if employment opportunities are limited. Increased regulation represents the most serious threat to the British economy's job-creating potential.

Cutting big business down to size
Red tape is suffocating enterprise. The Institute of Chartered Accountants of England and Wales estimates that compliance with regulation consumes 4–6% of the turnover of small employers.[9] 52% of employers have been required to hire a solicitor to deal with the complexities of employment law.[10] A survey of 1,300 employers by Peninsula found that three-quarters said that increased regulation over Labour's five years made it harder to start up a business.[11] This may be one of the

reasons why only 1 in 33 Britons are starting up new businesses compared with 1 in 10 citizens of the United States.[12] Graeme Leach, Chief Economist of the Institute of Directors has written:[13]

> The direct and indirect costs of regulation could be huge, amounting to 9% of GDP in the UK . . . The combined impact of public spending and regulation – the Intervention Index – is rapidly approaching 50% of GDP under New Labour.

But Labour is hiding the scale of the problem. Leach quotes the Minister for the Cabinet Office's answer to a question on the total compliance costs for UK businesses, in general, and businesses with fewer than 100 employees, in particular. The Minister replied: 'The government do not, and do not intend, to publish estimates in the form requested.'

The failure of business giants like Enron and WorldCom has led many on the Left to rush to declare a crisis of capitalism and to seek a battery of still more regulations. And some tougher laws are necessary – corrupt chief executives should be punished severely and, if necessary, jailed. But the growth of regulation has all the appearances of a cosy arrangement between big government and big business against the public interest. Many big businesses can live with regulation because they can afford to absorb it, but it makes it much more difficult for new players to challenge their market dominance. Increased regulation serves the political ambitions of the Left to rebuild the corporatism that so failed Britain during the 1970s. Neal Lawson of Renewal – 'a journal of Labour politics' – and a former aide to Gordon Brown has been honest enough to admit this ambition. Lawson recommends a corporatism that will control pay awards for chief executives and lift the pay of poorer workers. It would focus on environmental standards and 'seek consensus for seemingly intractable policy problems such as transport, housing and pensions'.[14] Big business would quickly become tools of government policy. Employers' administration of the Chancellor's highly complex system of tax credits is an early warning of things to come. The benefits of such corporatism would be hugely offset by the stagnating effect that this would have on the wealth-creating potential of the economy.

In opposing excessive regulation it is vital that Conservatives make it clear that we do so for reasons of public interest. As friends of capitalism Conservatives defend it from would-be oligopolists. That is why the second set of policy priorities in this essay involve (1) increased competition and (2) democratisation of political funding.

Wherever possible Conservatives should increase competition rather than increase regulation. This is particularly relevant to the crisis of confidence facing the financial sector. If small investors believe that accountancy firms, banks, chief executives and directors are all looking after themselves then they will walk away from the market. Irwin Stelzer, director of regulatory studies at the Hudson Institute, argues that the first priority should be to 'get the

incentives right'.[15] Auditors should be uninterested in the consequences of a tough but honest audit for their own company's
consultancy relationship with the object of their audit. Investment
analysts should rate a company accurately regardless of the implications for their own bank's business relationship with the
company in question. Stelzer recommends that instead of increasingly stringent policing of conflicts of interest within firms, such
conflicts should be removed altogether. Auditing firms should be
legally separated from consultancy arms, he suggests, and, because
chinese walls in banks between traditional bankers and analysts
often fail, these functions should be forcibly separated.

The principle of increasing competition could be more
widely applied but will not, of course, remove the need for regulation altogether. But a reversal of the regulatory juggernaut will
help ease the burden on small, community-based firms in particular and focus government on framing better, rather than more,
regulation.

An important dimension to a Conservative emphasis on
competition would be to break other links between big business
and big government. The link between big business and big
government is lubricated by big money and Conservatives should
advocate a cap on donations to political parties.[16] This would be a
powerful signal that Conservatives are directing our attention
away from big monied businesses towards a broader base of
support and perspective. The ugliest manifestations of the links
between big business and government are seen in high profile
cash-for-favours scandals but there are other, more insidious

consequences. This includes the growth of regulation that is advocated by well-connected and anti-competitive businesses.

We need to beware of politicians whose first instinct is to compensate for the problems in a system rather than to deal with the problems at their root. We see such a policy at work in the benefits system, where Gordon Brown is extending the terms of dependence rather than increasing independence. There is a parallel in the business sphere where a complex of regulatory structures is being built up to contain situations that should not exist in the first place. This is not just a parallel. The 'tax credit' bureaucracy that underpins Gordon Brown's benefits policy has been offloaded onto employers – an extra burden that will curtail the capacity of business, especially small business, to create the employment and self-employment opportunities by which the vulnerable might otherwise achieve independence. Where once the Left sought to seize the commanding heights of the economy, it now seeks to re-establish its power by setting up the state as the micromanager of weakness in the economy – whether those weaknesses be in the form of individual difficulties in finding a job or flaws in corporate governance. But in doing so, the state does not bring strength to anyone or anything but itself and its proxies; rather, weakness is cemented into the economy to the detriment of everyone else.

Extending opportunity again

Big businesses lobbying for regulations that act as barriers to the entry of smaller enterprises is not the only example of privileged and wealthy groups who favour limits on opportunity. The bureaucracy of the welfare state campaigns for the system's retention although it fails those it was intended to assist. The propertied and prosperous build walls to protect themselves from the anger of the left-behinds rather than seeking social and economic opportunity for children in the inner cities. Rich trading blocs like the EU sustain their agricultural industries by protectionism against African farmers.

We Conservatives have been at our best when we have been the party of hope and opportunity. We don't need to be embarrassed about wealth creation but we do need to be more articulate about its purpose. Again, this is nothing foreign to Margaret Thatcher's agenda. In 1998, albeit belatedly, she realised the dangers of not responding to the 'loadsamoney' critique of her policies and told the Church of Scotland:[17]

> It is not the creation of wealth that is wrong but love of money for its own sake. The spiritual dimension comes in deciding what one does with the wealth. How could we respond to the many calls for help, or invest for the future, or support the wonderful artists and craftsmen whose work also glorifies God, unless we had first worked hard and used our talents to create the necessary wealth?

The tragedy was that the four Conservative administrations of 1979–1997 were insufficiently active in defining and promoting a purpose for the prosperity that those years created. We could have done more to encourage a voluntary spirit of social engagement and philanthropy in British business, for example. Today's Conservatives need to embrace an opportunity agenda but – as essays in this book have argued – that cannot be done without a broader understanding of what motivates and nourishes people. Iain Duncan Smith talked about the shared successes of life in his introduction. Other chapters have demonstrated that many people – particularly vulnerable people – can only achieve independence and dignity through the active care of a diversity of people-sized institutions such as the family, local school and neighbourhood charity.[18]

The Conservative mission to renew society depends upon maintaining a growing economy. But that growing economy depends, in turn, upon a renewal of the values and institutions of society. It depends upon limits being placed on the threats to society and those threats come from big business as well as big government. And, most of all, the growing economy depends upon an extension of opportunity to the poor. Such a mission will not only sustain the whole nation's economic well-being but is also essential to human dignity, social justice[19] and the moral legitimacy of capitalism.

1   From Acceptance Speech to the Republican National Convention, 3 August 2000, Philadelphia

2   Address to Conservative Party workers by Edward Heath, 28 September 1973

3   In a speech to the Institute for Public Policy Research (IPPR) on 3 March 2002 Michael Howard vowed to defend this monetary policy regime from the uncertainty

Clifford Herbertson

of replacing it with oversight from the European Central Bank.

4   Iain Duncan Smith's private visit to FARE (Family Action on Rogerfield and Easterhouse) was made on 17 May 2002.

5   Speech to Conservative Christian Fellowship Scotland, Edinburgh, 10 May 2002

6   Lawrence M Mead, *The New Politics of Poverty: The Non-working Poor in America*, Basic Books, 1992

7   Ryan Streeter, *Transforming Charity: Towards a Results-Orientated Social Sector*, The Hudson Institute, 2001

8   For more information see www.corporate.servicemaster.com

9   ICA survey results, 12 October 2000.

10 *Sunday Telegraph*, 28 October 2001.

11 *Financial Times*, 25 April 2002.

12 Global Entrepreneurship Monitor, 2000 Executive Report.

13 In Blundell and Colin Robinson (eds), *Regulation Without the State... the Debate Continues*, Institute of Economic Affairs, November 2000

14 *New Statesman*, 29th July 2002.

15 'From 'Big Business' to 'Bad Behaviour'', *Weekly Standard*, 22 July 2002

16 A cap that would also apply to unions. The resulting likely reduction in funding of political parties could be compensated by matching every privately donated pound to a registered political party with a taxpayer-funded pound. Such a matching system would solve the funding crisis without entrenching incumbents.

17 Speech to the Church of Scotland General Assembly, Edinburgh, 21 May 1988

18 This was clearly the view of Brian Griffiths in 1985 when he delivered a speech entitled 'Monetarism and Morality' (The Second Patrick Hutber Memorial Lecture, 2 May 1985). Griffiths was concerned that 'the powerlessness of individuals in the inner city [was] at least partly the result of large government and the lack of mediating structures. I cannot understand why [the Bishop of Liverpool] and other church leaders advocate solutions which involve more public spending, bigger government, and our continued acceptance of the increasing politicisation of our lives – all of which tend to increase that feeling of powerlessness which he rightly identifies as dehumanising.'

19 Robin Harris – a senior aide to Margaret Thatcher – promoted a distinctively Conservative view of social justice and showed interest in the employment of that term in 'The Conservative Community: the roots of Thatcherism – and its future', a speech to the Centre for Policy Studies, 7 December 1989.

267

Postscript

Everyone is our neighbour

James Mawdsley

Pro-democracy campaigner James Mawdsley grew up in Lancashire, and now works in London for Christian Solidarity Worldwide. In 1999 he was arrested in Burma for the third time for challenging the military dictatorship and spent fourteen months as a prisoner of conscience. He is the author of The Heart Must Break, *an account of the struggle for democracy in Burma.*

In a recent speech, Caroline Spelman, the Shadow Secretary of State for International Development, proclaimed the Conservatives' identity as true internationalists:

> Our approach to the problems of the developing world should be practical. We should encourage independence not dependency. Give people the tools they need to lift themselves out of poverty. This means revamping debt relief and freeing world markets to make it easier for

poor countries to export their produce. Giving people a decent education because from education flows health, wealth and a real future. Currently every minute a woman dies while pregnant or giving birth in the Developing World, 7,000 people die of AIDS every day in Africa, 200 million Africans live on less than a dollar a day, a quarter of children in Afghanistan die before the age of five. We care about international development. And we have learnt from experience the cost of turning your back on a problem: in 1938 Neville Chamberlain famously described Czechoslovakia as 'the far away country of which we know little'. Conservatives must never be satisfied with knowing little.[1]

History makes it clear that threats to democracy anywhere are threats to democracy everywhere. However, the indivisibility of freedom holds true for the positive as well as the negative. This means that unless Britain actively supports democracy abroad then she is not going to have the sense or the opportunity to improve her own democracy at home. And the chief power to do this is not Britain's government. It is Britain's people.

Democracy, though, does not just mean elections and parliament. These are signs of democracy but the essence of it is participation, whereby citizens have maximum power to realise their aspirations, to exercise their free will in shaping their life and the life of their community and nation. Each person's power to do this increases as they enjoy increasing wealth, mobility, health, education and connections. When we have these we can defend ourselves from exploitation; we are free; our country is free.

There are deep reasons why we should defend and promote this true democracy abroad. There are also starkly obvious ones. To demonstrate the point I will outline five of the simplest: drugs, trade, immigration, environment and security.

Drugs

Most of the world's cocaine comes from Colombia, from territory controlled by the terrorist group FARC. Afghanistan, under the Taliban, used to be the world's foremost producer of heroin. Now it is Burma, a country ruled by tyrants. And Burma is also the world's foremost producer of methamphetamines. So long as tyrants, terrorists and warlords hold power, men with contempt for life and for the rule of law, then the supply of dangerous drugs will continue. And Britain suffers.

Trade

Prosperity is not limited to a finite pot over which nations must compete to maximise their share. Instead wealth begets wealth and peace allows it to multiply. If we wish to see international trade flourish, if we wish to maximise the benefit from all the talent, creativity and strength of six billion people, then we should wish to see an end to regimes that survive on corruption, exploitation and continual strife. Britain does most of her trade with other democracies, with countries that respect private property and the dignity of the labourer. As democracy spreads, wealth will grow.

Immigration

Immigration benefits every country that is open to it. Illegal immigration, though, is a curse. The social consequences are bad enough – fear, hostility and division. But the tragedy is in the smuggling, in the exploitation of people who are desperate to find security. In June 2000, 58 Chinese people suffocated in one truck travelling through the Channel Tunnel. Others, from Afghanistan, Iraq, Sudan and elsewhere, are drowned or electrocuted as they attempt to enter the UK. Why? For what are people willing to risk their lives? It is for rule of law – a concept and practice that is profoundly precious, especially to those escaping from repressive regimes. The solution to this disaster does not lie within Britain. It lies in defending everywhere fundamental human rights and in supporting the establishment of the rule of law. In a democratic world, illegal immigration would not be as big a problem.

Environment

Our most committed efforts to protect the environment will be ineffectual so long as citizens and communities in the Third World are denied their voice. There are 2.3 billion people in China and India alone, and they are just beginning to pollute in a way we mastered 150 years ago. The resultant pollution is set to increase incalculably and controlling it is not, at present, a priority of Third World powers. All environmental movements are bottom-up. They are powered from the grassroots. But whereas the majority of, say, Chinese and Indian people do not want to live with pollution any more than we do, they have few means and ways to challenge the established order. In Britain we still produce vast amounts of pollution and therefore it is hypocritical for us not to get our own house in order. However, getting our house in order will be a waste of time if the majority of people in the world have neither voice nor muscle to order theirs.

Security

Our country and our way of life at home are never safe so long as there is tyranny and the rule of might abroad. The greatest threats to global security come from totalitarian regimes themselves or from countries so lawless that terrorists can operate freely within them. All people are equal but political systems are not. A system that believes in the dignity of man and the rule of law must fight for its place in the world – or else it will be overwhelmed. And as it holds these values, then it must fight in a manner that does not violate them, or else it has already lost. We exercise and promote freedom, or we lose it.

If it is clear that it is in Britain's most vital interests to support democracy abroad, the challenge is to work out how we can effectively do that, and the fact that Britain has a flourishing democracy indicates by definition that the balance of power in our society lies with the citizens, not with the government. And thus if one of Britain's tasks is to support democracy abroad then it seems obvious that the task cannot be left only to government, but must be taken up by citizens.

What is preventing individual British people from spending six months to a year in the developing world? While there they could teach IT, or law, or medicine, or English, or engineering, or journalism. Communities in the developing world are desperate for this knowledge. Why don't we share it?

If an oppressed group is trying to get its message heard by the international community then the ability to speak English, the international lingua franca, is an enormous advantage; because who else can articulate their situation with as much authority as they can? With as much conviction, and accuracy, and understanding? Speaking English gives one a more powerful voice.

And the Internet is an incredible tool for undermining oppressive regimes. Regimes which rightly fear the Internet are still driven to encourage it because they dream of its economic fruits. But totalitarianism absolutely depends upon isolating people from each other and cutting them off from the outside world. The Internet will rip them apart.

Then there is law. There are plenty of regimes that have sound laws on their books but which flout these with impunity. This impunity is assured so long as few of their citizens are familiar with the law. And in countries where policemen and judges do not even understand, never mind respect, basic due process, then the law actually becomes a weapon to be used against people. Yet there is no regime in the world that admits to trampling on law. So, local lawyers, with crowds of supporters, could begin winning 'trivial' civil cases against petty officials. As the principle of law then becomes more widely appreciated, it is likely that cases which are more politically significant could then be won, with crucial scrutiny from the outside world giving protection to the lawyers and their supporting crowds. Blow by blow, justice is established.

Media coverage acts like a spotlight under which even tyrants are afraid to do wrong. So where there are people fighting to defend their families and their land from murderous regimes, then given the right training and equipment, perhaps one in ten of these soldiers could take a video camera on patrol instead of a rifle. The resulting footage, and documentaries, would make prime-time TV in the West and the response would be tremendous. We have the technology; they have the access. Our combined efforts would penetrate the most closed of countries.

Blankets and food can be dropped from the air in sacks. Knowledge and training cannot. They require real people, and lots of them, to be on the ground. There are countless people volunteering to do this already, and disproportionate numbers of them are students and pensioners as both groups are largely unconstrained by careers, mortgages and children. Youth has the gift of energy and idealism. Age offers experience and gentleness.

Costs are minimal – £2,000 covers six months in Africa or India. And even if individuals have difficulty in raising funds then communities here – churches, universities, associations – could raise funds to send a couple of their number to live abroad for a period. They could pack their envoys off with books, medicine, cash and computers. The envoys would then live as the locals live, very simply, and share their knowledge. When they returned they could give presentations to their backers and write articles for local newspapers, thus increasing realism at home. They could then invite two of their former hosts to spend time in the UK to give similar presentations and also to learn about life here. The following year, a different couple might go out. Over time solid relations would build up. It is these connections and relations, this understanding and knowledge, which will free people from exploitation.

But a most compelling reason for all this is that it will be of the greatest benefit to the one who seeks to serve others. Whoever spends six months in the developing world is going to learn some vital lessons from the local people: lessons in resilience, humility, hospitality, deference, simplicity. These values are immeasurably important to the development of the individual and to the health of society. Of course established democracies have much to offer financially, technologically and in legal expertise. But areas of the world blighted by material poverty often abound in richness of soul. We should not envisage one side 'giving' to the other; rather envisage people sharing their strengths to help others in their weakness. The concept is as old as society. The context and scale are as new as the day.

To illustrate this exchange of benefits more specifically: in refugee camps around the world parents are desperate for their children to receive an education and children are astonishingly keen to learn. Would it not then be a more meaningful endeavour for a British teacher to educate people who turn up to lessons early, who do all their homework, who value the chance to learn and who show loving respect to their teacher – rather than dodging chairs thrown at them by pupils in Britain?

Would it not be more satisfying for a lawyer to work on the release of political prisoners than to litigate over the inch-perfect placing of an obnoxious client's garden fence? Would life not be incalculably more rewarding for a doctor who saved lives and limbs abroad rather than performed cosmetic surgery at home? Or who would prefer to spend time honing their skills with computer games, if they had the chance of introducing a whole village to the Internet?

And what about university students? How many young people in Britain today go to college to study a subject they do not like for the reward of an academically dubious degree that employers don't rate and, even worse, a mountain of debt that robs them of their freedom for years? Would they not learn more spending a year in a developing country teaching IT or English? Surely it is in Britain's interests to have thousands returning home every month being braver, kinder, more humble and more realistic people than they were when they set out?

There are hundreds of non-government organisations already making all of this happen. The specific role of government would be to so encourage appropriate schemes as to make this part of our national culture. For example they could give respected accreditation to facilitating organisations, and host a single website featuring all these groups and the multifarious types of placements they offer. DfID could encourage tremendous participation by match-funding applicants up to an agreed ceiling. Surely this is better than the current system of granting huge sums of aid to corrupt and repressive governments? School career advisers could promote the option. Yet it would be vital that government did not try to take the scheme over; such an attempt would destroy it.

The most fundamental role of government would be to provide two essentials: freedom and leadership. Freedom for citizens means a light state, because there must be no fiscal, cultural or political obstacles to deter people from participation. A political party that is afraid to devolve freedom to its citizens is not fit to govern.

However, freedom can be abused, so leadership too is required. But leadership does not mean management. Instead leadership requires that individuals within government believe that every human person has an inherent and inalienable dignity, that all people deserve to be free from fear and oppression, and that we can never be whole or complete, save at the service of our neighbour. If these are true here, then they are true everywhere. And if politics is not for people, it is not for anything.

---

1   Caroline Spelman, speech to the Conservative Party Spring Forum, Harrogate, 24 March 2002